My Piano
My Life

The Life of Jacqueline Gourdin
as told to
Robert Erickson

Robert Erickson

Goose River Press
Waldoboro, Maine

bobericksonwriter@yahoo.com

Library of Congress Card Number 2010928403

ISBN: 9781597131018

Cover design by Brenda Erickson

Other writings by Robert Erickson:

Snooky, Recollections of a Boy from Skokie
The Poetry of a Life in Maine

Published, Goose River Anthology, 2008, 2009, 2010

Published by
Goose River Press
3400 Friendship Road
Waldoboro, ME 04572-6337
gooseriverpress@roadrunner.com
www.gooseriverpress.com

To my father

MY PIANO MY LIFE

Prologue

Portland, Maine is an old port town located about a hundred miles northeast of Boston. It was in it's glory during the whaling period of New England history when the tall masted sailing ships set sail around the horn bound for the prolific whaling waters off San Francisco and Alaska, filling their holds with the oil that lighted the lamps of the western world. The ships sailed for years at a time, many carrying the whale oil to the far eastern ports of China and Malaysia, returning with the spices of the Orient to be sold in America or England and Spain. Portland thrived during this great era of sail. Maine timber provided masts for most of the sailing ships of the time and shipbuilding became a major industry down east. But the age of sail gave way at the turn of the century to the steam engine vessels developed during the Industrial Revolution. The beautiful, pristine wharfs of the eighteen hundreds gave way to the oil and coal of the new century and the shops and industrial buildings lining Commercial Street degraded to greasy bars and brothels. It became a red light district catering to the sailors of the world while Portland struggled with decay.

Today Portland is the financial and cultural capitol of the state and has risen from the ashes of an irrelevant waterfront ghetto during the first half of the twentieth century to a renovated, rejuvenated cultural center where industry and art flourish together. Commercial Street is clean and vibrant with nautical businesses, upscale shops and restaurants lining the wharfs while the Old Port section, with its old brick, wrought iron, narrow streets and quaint boutiques, remind us of its heritage. Artists and musicians display their crafts in the small parks amidst the granite gray office buildings of Congress Street and the financial district; a strange combination of Birkenstocks and dark blue suits. This is the city to which Jacqueline Gourdin brought her music and her life.

The night was a sultry but beautiful evening which was typical of Maine in August. We could smell the harbor but there was no sea breeze that night so it was a steaming harbor we sensed; hot, humid with nothing moving but the slow tide. We had parked our car a few blocks from the music studio and walked eagerly but slowly, having arrived early for the performance. Children were playing in the streets and on the sidewalks which were lined with young maples that arched over the walkway giving the air the unusual combined fragrance of green growth and hot concrete. My wife and I talked about Jacqui as we strolled; our beautiful Jacqui, recalling the events that had brought her to Portland just months before; events that might have emotionally crippled the faint of heart; events that would certainly have destroyed a music career and yes, maybe even a life. Portland was her goal, it always had been, even the many years before when she lived in Dorchester, a suburb of Boston, where we had first met her and where the emancipation of Jacqueline Gourdin had begun.

The studio was small and filled to capacity. The air conditioners labored to keep the hall cool but with limited success as several women used the concert program as a fan. Peoples' faces shined with the warmth but also with delight looking to the night's performance. As the lights dimmed the audience hushed in anticipation of an unusual recital featuring one piano-four hands. A gentleman stood on the stage and simply announced, "Ladies and gentlemen, Jacqueline Gourdin." And Jacqui took the stage to great applause. This petite lady in her sixties who couldn't have stood more than five feet one or two walked to her piano and placed a hand on the open side of the grand as though she were caressing something alive. She wore a simple light blue dress that complimented the blue wall color, her grey hair was pulled back in a bun which was part of her signature appearance and her mocha skin was aglow with pleasure and the night. There was a slight smile that exuded confidence and pleasure at once, a smile with which we were so familiar that said, "This is my domain, this is where I belong and you will see why." She didn't speak immediately, which was a practiced part of her stage presence that held the attention of everyone in the hall. First she made eye contact, looking at each row as though she personally knew each person there. She thanked all for coming in her soft, controlled stage voice that almost had a lilt of British; but no, more like the voice and diction of live theater. Then Jacqui, with a broad smile, introduced her four hand partner for the evening, Keith Witherell. Keith walked briskly to Jacqui and bowed to the crowd. He was a big man who seemed an unlikely pianist who overemphasized Jacqui's petiteness but a person and partner in whom Jacqui had complete confidence and respect. Keith was a product of Jacqui's tutelage starting his piano career with Jacqui at the age of seven and studying with her for eleven years before going on to his bachelors and masters degrees in music. Teacher and pupil were totally at ease as they sat at the bench and made several adjustments to accommodate the disparity in size; Keith to the treble side and Jacqui to the bass. The music was to begin.

The concert started with Variations by Beethoven which was received with thunderous applause, then a piece by Faure, Dolly Suite then The Shubert Variations that was brilliant and the evening was to be complete with the Grande Sonata in F Minor, Opus 178 by Czerny. The Sonata began very melodious and the two pianists swayed to the rhythm almost as though they were somehow joined at the side. Jacqui turned the pages as necessary with the practiced hand of someone who had done so thousands of times; a flicking motion that never missed the page and was done so quickly that there was no interruption in her score. They were in true concert with each other as the tempo began to rise from adagio to the cut time finale. Their fingers seemed to fly over the keyboard in crescendo after crescendo as the swells of music grew more and more intense. Jacqui played with such force that the piano almost seemed to quiver under her fingers. I could feel the music reverberate in my chest as they gave their whole being to each musical swell. I watched our dear friend actually come off the bench as she struck one of the final chords. Her eyes were riveted to the score and the final notes were struck in perfect unison. Then it was over. The silence was an awesome contrast to that wonderful finale. In that silence there was a surprised pause. It was as if the audience was reeling from the emotion of the music from which they had to recover. And recover they did with tremendous applause, whistles and cries of "Bravo, Bravo." The two performers bowed and bowed to hands that would not stop their appreciation and despite their exhaustion played another short selection to show appreciation. While they were playing I reflected on the life that brought Jacqui to this place, to this level of excellence; one which started in the ashes of black poverty and persistently struggled to self actualization, success and fulfillment. Maybe that is why she loves Portland so much; they are very much alike.

Chapter 1

I was born in Sarasota, Florida. I'm sure that Sarasota is a wonderful place. Oddly enough it was discovered and then conceived in Scotland in 1885 and settled by Scottish and English immigrants by simply moving the Seminole Indians out. From everything I have heard it has beautiful citrus groves, clean streets and wonderful waterways that attract the money people every winter; the people with two homes or recreation vehicles who also tow large white boats that fill the inlets and those waterways. They come from everywhere and you can tell by the license plates that these are people escaping the cold of the north from Chicago, from New York, Boston or Cleveland. I can just imagine what it is like because I see so much here in Maine during the summers when the people "from away" cram the highways and coastal roads seeking to escape the heat of the South or Midwest to find a cool beach on the coast in their recreation vehicles towing the same white boats with the same license plates. They are vacation people in reverse seeking the sun and spending all that money for leisure time. Mostly white people as far as I can see and I think it is the same in Sarasota. I can only imagine that it was the same in Sarasota when I was born but I don't really know because I can't remember it. I was very young when we left.

I was born on December third, nineteen hundred and thirty five but I didn't even know that until I was over sixty years old. People can't understand how in the world you couldn't know when you were born but that's because they are not black and were not born in the Deep South. They could never find my damn birth certificate because some dumb-assed midwife delivered me at home and then went to her home and registered my birth in another county. Not only that but people never kept any bloody records. Somebody's born? Somebody's born! Big deal! End of report!

The only thing I know about it is what my mother told me and that was pretty limited because there was a great deal that my mother would rather not tell me, and didn't. There was some talk that my people started out in Georgia but I don't know any details. I think it was better to be black in Sarasota than in Georgia but it was hard being black anywhere in nineteen thirty five. We are talking only about seventy years and maybe three generations after the freeing of the slaves in this country. The word "free" was truly stretching the meaning of the word and "segregation" was only a modified form of slavery. Separate bathrooms, dining rooms, restaurants, water fountains, motels, hotels and stores. My people were offered only menial jobs with low expectations and no real opportunity and, on occasion, brutality was the "freedom" most blacks knew back then.

My mother's name is Willie Pearl Palmer and that was the family name; my grandmother's name was Palmer, but I don't know anything about my father. I only know what was told to me and much of that is questionable, as I don't know what was truth or fiction. His name was supposed to be James Massey and I was told that he passed away when I was very young, an infant. I don't know if he ever even saw me but the hardest part is that I don't know the truth about it. I can find no written record about him. There is, however, something inside of me that says I need to know who he was and I have a very strong goal in life to find him. One way or the other I will.

Most people can trace their genealogy because of the family unit, family records, family Bibles and public archives. Tracing a Negro family, however, is very difficult because of the very nature of slavery. The actual concept of family was destroyed by the slave boats and auction blocks. Slave traders, brokers and owners broke up any family relationships to keep total control of the individual. An auction was synonymous with the breaking up of families and it wasn't limited just to the adults. Brothers and sisters were bid off first and to the mother's paralyzing grief, even infants were sold to the highest bidder. Men and women were bought for breeding purposes; the men for their physiques and ability to work and the women for their ability to bear many children. A slave would not even stay on one plantation for long. Most lived on several in their lifetimes. But "living" is not a proper term; "existing" would be better. For the most part slaves were housed in mere shacks with dirt floors, leaky roofs, drafty walls and beds made out of nothing more than a wide board with a piece of wood for a pillow and maybe rags for bedclothes. Not all plantation owners were cruel but many were and the major form of punishment was the whip. Many times the offense was merely that a slave looked at a white woman too long or that he didn't "Yes ma'am" or that he wasn't working hard enough. It sometimes took weeks for the poor wretch to recover from such a horrible mauling and the stripes on his back were constant reminders of what it was like to be owned by another.

The reason for this inhumanity was that these people were considered "things," things to toil in the fields, cook the meals, cut wood and whatever else was determined by an owner, including making more babies for the next generation of "things." Although these poor, miserable people felt the same emotions of joy, sorrow, love and anger as their owners, they were treated as dumb brutes incapable of anything beyond working, reproducing, singing and dancing. And they didn't know where they came from just as their children would never know. Is it any wonder that seventy years or so later I would be brought into the world by someone I might never know.

The concept of being a father was, and still is in some ways, difficult for some black men. The result of slavery was that there was no legality, no traditions and no family values. Working at a nothing job and making babies were the best of their expectations and the concept of one wife and the white picket fence just didn't fit. I don't know whether James Massey and mother were married or not but it was rumored that he had had another child up the street so obviously James Massey got around. He was also known to be quite light skinned and maybe had some Indian blood in his background. Maybe that is why I am lighter than most, but on the other hand, that is what I had also heard about my grandfather. That is all hearsay and rumor. I do remember them telling me though, that whatever heritage my father bore, I came out looking too white and I had to be hidden because in those days if a black woman produced a baby like I looked, she had been dealing with a white man and that was against the rules.

Color was always a big issue in our culture and in our house. My mother told me that one time I contracted yellow Jaundice and that I was so yellow I shone in the dark. Supposedly my grandmother went out in the yard and picked roots of some sort, boiled them in a pot and fed them to me for several days. A "sugar tit" they called it and in a few days I returned to my normal color. Whatever that concoction was, it did its work.

There is something I do know about my father though, it is that he watches over me and has since his death. I didn't come to realize that for many years but I know he is in my life. On several occasions I have gone to psychics and in each case they have mentioned a man, a little man on my left or right. It is the first thing they would mention. People don't have to believe all this but I do, it works for me and I believe that my father takes care of me still. I ask my father, in my head, why in the hell didn't you stay here? Why did you have to go there to take care of me? Why didn't you stay here? But all of this is in the past and some day I'll see him. Not in this dimension, but we will be together and I'm dying to see him and when the time comes I'll be ready.

Women are the strength of the black family and I was brought up by women. Grandmother's name was Mariah Palmer and I remember seeing her on several occasions. She had seventeen babies in clumps. She would have three or four and then a space, then three of four more. My mother and three sisters were one "clump." Grandmother, God save her, was not a nice person. If there was something you said that she didn't like, that arm would fly out and you would pick yourself up off the floor. Violence seemed to run very deep in my family. I don't know why it was but they were just argumentative. I grew up with language that would make a coal miner blush particularly when they were arguing, so my vocabulary of dirty words was complete at an early age. I'm afraid they were just not very happy people.

My mother, Willie, whom they also called "Sweets" was third in line. Birdell was the oldest, then Hazel and the youngest, Lee. We all lived together and Birdell was the strongest of them all, and I mean strong. Birdell told everyone what to do, she was the head honcho and very violent. When I say violent, I don't mean a few little arguments or a few cross words. I mean knock down, drag out, break your arms, black your eyes violence. She was a big woman with thunderous thighs and breasts and clearly ruled the roost with an iron fist and a big stick. In my recollection of being a youngster, what stands out the most, unfortunately, is the violence. I was always fearful of someone getting killed because she was a highly combative person. She was a man in a woman's body and I was afraid of her and so were my mother and the other sisters as well as the several husbands and other men she brought home.

We all lived in the same house and Aunt Birdell had a son named Jessie. Jessie was the first male I remember in my life and I sort of loved and respected him. He was five years older than I and for years I thought he was my brother. As a matter of fact I called Birdell, "Mummy" and my own mother, "Mother" not really understanding the difference. It was the only family unit we had and I was too young to understand that it was supposed to be any other way. Jessie and I became very close and we clung to each other as the violence raged. I was never physically beaten by Birdell but Jessie was and he was scared to death of his mother. Mother would protect Jessie and would physically stand between him and the beatings.

Mummy was so strong that she commanded the entire house. She spoke with authority and took care of everything to the point that she stole my mother's identity and her ability to function except in a small area of her life. Mother was a very small woman, almost frail and she felt she had been cheated from being a mother because Birdell's word was final in all matters. Therefore I had a surrogate mother and a brother who was really a cousin and a real mother who was becoming tired of being put upon. All I knew as a little girl is that mother was very upset and I cried; I cried a great deal.

When I was born my mother was supposed to have been married to a man by the name of Mr. Jones. However, Mr. Jones was in prison having committed some very naughty crime. The law said at that time that if a husband was in prison for seven years or more, you were no longer married. It was while he was in prison that mother became pregnant by James Massey. Mr. Jones was the size of England and as black as the ace of spades. As I mentioned, when I arrived, I was quite light in color, too white. I might as well have had blonde hair and blue eyes and in those days if a black woman had been dealing with a white man, and as I have said, it was a definite no-no. I was clearly not the offspring of Mr. Jones so I was kind of hidden away, not taken to many places outside of the house. The story is that my mother wanted to marry my father, James Massey but he had supposedly passed away when I was an infant, or so the story goes. Willie knew one thing, she knew she had better get her ass out of there before that big, black Mr. Jones was let out of jail and set his eyes on me. Nevertheless she gave me the name of Jones, Jacqueline Jones.

Chapter 2

One day the sisters announced that we were moving north. Ah yes, North to the "Promised Land" of better employment, higher wages and much improved working conditions. The migration from the south had been going on for decades and had started during slavery with the advent of the Underground Railroad where runaway slaves were harbored in attics, fruit cellars and hay stacks and who were nurtured by free blacks and whites alike as the pursued fled for the promises of the north. The horrors of enslavement drove people to acts of sheer desperation as they tried to evade the owners and their dogs who all too frequently would capture and drag the poor escapee back to the plantation where he or she was made an example with the whip and other forms of torture. Those who made it to the northern, industrial states and beyond to Canada in fact found better lives. Not great lives but better.

One classic story is told about a black slave who was nailed into a wooden crate and "mailed" to Boston. After three days by sea and rail he arrived to the astonishment of the postal clerk who heard his cries of agony and joy. Other stories told of well-to-do white women, opposed to slavery, who would take female slaves posing as servants on trips north and then release them at their destinations. These stories got back to those remaining and more and more slaves followed the Underground Railroad. The promises of the Promised Land were becoming real.

Emancipation started an ever increasing migration to the north where there were jobs but racism and segregation prevented much of an improvement in income. The jobs available for blacks were menial at best and, again, mostly domestic and physical in nature. But these migrants were at least free and after 1920 blacks were allowed to vote and the numbers of migrants were developing black neighborhoods in large cities where sheer numbers were creating improved life styles. The advent of World War I created new factory positions in defense plants manufacturing war machines and equipment. Although discrimination was still rampant the manpower requirement was so great that employers had no choice. Soon blacks were starting to occupy "white" jobs such as secretaries and clerks and sales people. Racial bigotry was still prevalent but things were starting to improve. That is what Birdell, Hazel and Sweets had learned and were ready to jump onto their own Railroad.

One of the main reasons for moving north was Mr. Jones. Mother was a very small woman and Elmo Jones was a large man with hands like sides of beef. She was afraid that when he got out of prison and saw me he would turn on her and God knows what he would have done. I keep thinking of the Shaking Baby Syndrome. He could shake her like a doll and she was sure he would do it too. The other issue that prompted all the women to make the move was that it was an opportunity to leave the bondage of the south behind. That Railroad to the north meant a great deal to women who were in search of more work and more pay. They were convinced as a result of everything they had heard that life was better and freer in the north. I think Birdell had known someone who had moved to Boston and so that's where she was headed with Sweets, Jessie and me in tow. Hazel, on the other hand, had heard all about New York. Hazel was a real piece of work. To her, everything was all glitz. She was always over dressed and used a tremendous amount of makeup and jewelry and all she would talk about were the bright lights on Harlem. She was about as big as Birdell and almost as violent. The whole neighborhood knew it when she and Birdell got into a fight. It was truly the survival of the fittest because Birdell was just a little bit bigger and a little bit meaner than Hazel so she was still the dominant authority. She used to call herself the "HNIC," which translated into Head Nigger In Charge. Mother was timid and cowered before both of them. Lee was indecisive and had something going with her new-found boyfriend and had decided to stay in Sarasota. That was the last close contact I ever had with my Aunt Lee.

So three of the Palmer girls packed up and left Florida for their own Promised Lands. Birdell, Willie, Jessie and I were on our railroad tracks to Boston and Hazel on her tracks to New York. I can't really remember the details of that move but it was one of the most formative things that ever happened to me. Jesse and I were excited but scared to death.

Hello Cambridge, Massachusetts! This was a hell of a lot different from little old Sarasota, Florida. Mother and Birdell found a house on Hancock Street. It was on a hill between Harvard Square and Central Square. I remember we weren't allowed to play in the street because the cars would rush down that hill very fast so we had to play on the sidewalk. It was a busy place and I don't remember my family having any neighborly relationships with other people. It was a mixed neighborhood because my aunt and mother didn't want to be with only blacks. After all we had left the south to get away from the southern, all black influence. Birdell never let us forget that she brought us north to better ourselves, to get a good education, to learn etiquette, to become as white and sophisticated as we could become; and to get rid of our goddamned southern black accents. There was no way we could drag out our pronunciations. We were not to sound black and that is why, today, I speak so bloody clean. The schools I went to spoke very, very proper English. So between Birdell and school, we spoke good, clear English.... or else.

All of the women in our house worked as domestics in rich peoples' homes. That's what black women in the South did for work, either domestic or physical. They were either washing clothes or dishes, cleaning house, cooking and looking after the owners' children or more physical labor like working in the fields, stemming tobacco leaves or plucking chickens. Birdell was a horribly violent person but not at the homes she now worked in. She was the picture of the obedient and dedicated servant but it was all an act. She simply manipulated these white folks to get what she wanted and she did it well. She also adopted their personal traits; her diction was perfect, almost to the point of being theatrical. She could talk like a black as we all could, and did, at home. There were two languages, the very southern black dialect and the white, perfect King's English used in front of her employers and in stores where she didn't know anyone. She could switch back and forth depending on her surroundings. It is called "shifting" and it carries on today. She did not dress as a domestic when she went to work as she was impeccably attired, scrubbed squeaky clean, conservatively perfumed and from the time she left the door she held her head in a most aristocratic manner. From the waist up, Birdell was royalty and her employer families loved it. She had it down pat and she expected us to know how to do it too. To this day, although I feared and hated her as a child, I can attribute my personal demeanor to much of what she taught and demanded of me. When she came home, however, it was a remarkable transformation. That demure attitude disappeared as the home door slammed and she became Aunt Birdell once again. She had shifted all right and we had better have done all we were supposed to or there was hell to pay. That went for everyone in the house and especially my mother "Sweets" who was not so sweet as she was scared shitless of her sister.

The Palmer women had moved to Massachusetts for the reasons I mentioned but I must repeat that mother was very afraid of Mr. Jones. She was also sick and tired of Birdell so she decided to find a man. She corresponded through the Lonely Hearts Club in the local newspaper and lo and behold, who arrived on the scene but Mr. Fontaine, Mr. James Fontaine who after a short and torrid relationship, married Willie and he became my instant stepfather. I think they got married but I don't know for sure. Fontaine came from Delaware and was a foster child having been raised by an uncle and aunt and had had a horrible upbringing. He was very black, almost blue-black and he had wonderfully smooth skin. He was a good looking and dapper gentleman but he had an unfortunate stutter. The more excited he got, the more he stuttered. Willie, of course was controllingly relentless with him because while James was trying to get something out past his stutter, Willie would recite chapter and verse and by the time James recovered, the conversation was over. To my surprise Fontaine was really nice to me and I liked him a lot. I guess all I said when I met him was, "Hello, I understand you are going to be my daddy." You see, he was the first daddy that I had ever known. "Yes I am," he replied and we got along very well from that moment on.

Birdell hated James Fontaine and called him a 'little son-of-a-bitch' to his face. She looked at him as a threat and she had never let any man threaten her and her iron clad control. He was miserable living in the same house with her so mother and Fontaine decided to move out and relocate to Delaware. It was where he had come from so he was confident there was good work and they could start anew. They were employed by the same family; she as a maid and he as a butler. I had been put in some sort of a day care situation. It is all a blur to me I was so young but for some reason it didn't work out.

Mother always seemed to be getting sick and she was not happy so we loaded up again and returned to the Boston area. They got their own place and James and Willie worked for families again as house help of one kind or another. One thing about James was that he always had a steady job and was a fairly good provider for that reason. Mother found a position with a Jewish family with whom she was to develop a long-standing relationship.

I was old enough now where I had to make some social adjustments. I didn't have a lot of friends and especially not female friends. I never had girls over for the night, because with my mother, there was always fear of the sexual thing. I liked boys a lot more anyway but there was certainly the sexual inference there too. But I would much rather have a bunch of boys around me and I got along with them in a minute. However there was one boy who made a big mistake. He told me that Jessie was not my brother and he explained the relationship difference. God rest his soul, I beat the begeesit out of him. The poor baby, I tried to crucify him right there on the sidewalk. "Don't you tell me he isn't my brother, you son of a bitch," I screamed. He ran. God how he ran! I do know that, as a child, I was a fighter from the word go. I guess I know where I got that from! I would fight anybody you put in front of me if I had to and as a matter of fact I think I would rather fight than do anything else at that point in my life. I became better at relationships later on but learning that Jessie wasn't my brother devastated me as a child.

I loved Jessie dearly and we were very close. He was older than I but you know me, the flippant, mouthy one and as far as I was concerned we were on an even keel; I was as good as he was and whatever he wanted to do, so did I. I started off in dancing and ballet and I really liked it and I was going great guns but I was anemic and it was a physical overload, or at least so said the doctor. "Anemic," that was the magic word in those days. On the doctor's recommendation, I was to give up dancing. Birdell had learned of a contest to discover piano talent. I was entered into the contest because I had been copying Jessie's piano lessons and could play a limited amount. I won the contest on artistic potential and received a five-year scholarship for piano lessons. It was at that point I took up the piano and although I didn't know it then, I had begun the journey down the road to the passion of my life. And it was ok with me at that point because Jessie was playing piano and whatever Jessie did, I was going to do.....and better. Little did I know what that was going to mean to me.

With that five-year scholarship mother didn't have to pay the fifty cents per lesson normally charged. I liked going to the lessons but I wasn't very impressed with my teacher who was not very disciplined. She had extremely long fingernails and consequently couldn't even play the piano. Later on I discovered that all her diplomas were highly suspect and she had built all the hoopla about her over the fact that she was the first black to do this and the first black to do that. I don't buy that shit. She represented herself as a graduate of the New England Conservatory but I doubt if any of that was true because in those days, there may have been three or four blacks as graduates but believe me, she wasn't one of them. That inadequate training would live with me forever.

I loved playing the piano and I, being the big mouth, took over the studio. I was the star pupil. I played and played and played but without direction. I just don't remember any discipline. She would spend her time on the telephone and drinking tea while I just played and played. People call it practicing when you sit at the piano and play and play but that's not true. We have to be taught how to practice and we have to

Jacqueline Jones, age 5½ when she started piano lessons with Anna Bobitt-Gardner, Mus. B.

Jacqueline Jones, at the close of her musical training with Anna Bobitt-Gardner, Mus. B. before she entered Boston Conservatory of Music

learn how to stay with a piece with a tremendous amount of repetition before we move on to something else. I must have been very good because I remember many recitals and everyone in the family was very supportive. I was Jacqueline, the beautiful little child sitting at the piano in her pinafore and patten leather shoes, smiling demurely at the parents assembled, playing better than anyone my age because I worked at it. I was absorbed in the music; my piano was rapidly becoming something I needed; I had to play. I practiced every day and I copied all the pieces that Jessie was playing because I wanted to be better than him even though he was older. I wanted to be the best there was and the piano had become my social life, my friend, my mentor and my frustration outlet when the household was out of control.

Edwards, Jr. and Sr. on Guard duty

When I was about eleven, Daddy would take me to his National Guard Armory drills. Every Wednesday night Fontaine would dress me up in army fatigues and I would put my braids up on top of my head and I would go and watch all the soldiers marching. I felt so big and important to be the only girl there but there was another kid attending who was the commanding officer's son. He was my age and his name was Edward Gourdin, Jr. Daddy introduced me and I liked him immediately. He was kind of a little guy which was strange because his father, Colonel Edward Gourdin, was tall and stately and had that military bearing that commanded immediate respect. He had a lot of ribbons on his chest and he was the commander of the 372nd all black Artillery Unit and everyone knew it because he was giving the orders and I thought that was really neat. I always looked forward to going on Wednesday nights to see the soldiers do their drills but also to see Edward. I thought he was really neat too.

As I grew older and more independent, I started to take on the same traits as Mother and Mummy but fortunately for me I had a channel to put all that energy into. Otherwise I would be out there punching people out and putting them up against the wall one minute, then schmoozing the white folks, like Birdell, to save a shitty job, the next. I didn't have any sisters to fight with so I went to the piano and that is truly a good thing because it kept me out of the street. But it kept me from normal interaction with people so that by the time I was out in society I was horribly ill prepared. I really didn't know how to react. I had school but my piano was far more important. It was quickly becoming my life and I was withdrawing into it.

Mother was putting up barriers for James Fontaine, barriers he was not to cross. Because of all the hanky panky she had seen in the south, she was very leery of him in relation to me as I was reaching puberty and was starting to look like more than the little girl he first knew. He treated me as a father would and never made any improper moves on me at all. I think I would have known if he had. I knew the ropes. I thought he was a good man and we respected and liked each other a great deal so I never worried.....but Willie did.

Fontaine was pretty good to Mother at the start but while she went to work and spent it on the house, he would go out and drink and spend it on having a good time. If Mother had been a little more feminine, a little smoother, a soft caring wife, I think he would have stayed around more. But the fights would start about money and then out he would go and drink and she became less attentive and he became more scarce. After a while it got pretty bad and he would put us out of the house. They would have a knock down drag out fight and Mother and I would throw some clothes into brown paper bags and we would go to Birdell's house until everything blew over. Birdell's house for God sakes! Of all the places she hated to go but it was the only place she could go to get away from the fighting and the violence. From the frying pan to the fire. A little smoothing over and back we would go, brown bags and all. Mother, on the other hand didn't know how to smooth anything over and after a while we stopped leaving at all. Mother was really between a rock and a hard place; scared to death of Birdell and pissed at Fontaine.

One year Fontaine brought me a bicycle for my birthday. It was a beautiful Schwinn bike with a very shiny coat of paint, all green and white. It had balloon tires and I would ride it every day and it was the one thing that I had that other kids envied. It was the only thing in my life at that time that had real meaning, except for my piano, of course. I remember the horror of walking home from school one day and seeing my bicycle in the pawnshop window. My bike! I couldn't believe it! I ran the rest of the way and cried until Mother got home and I told her and all she could say was that he needed his alcohol. You needed your alcohol did you Mr. Fontaine? How much did you buy with my bicycle? Did you offer your bar buddies a drink and say, "Here pal, have a pedal, here sweetheart, have a wheel. Here's a tip bartender, have a fender?"

James Fontaine was the only father I ever knew and I couldn't just throw him away like a used paper plate but I was terribly hurt. I had lost what affection I ever had for him and yet I felt strangely guilty about my anger. And he knew because if looks could kill, he would have been dead meat. My real father would never have done anything like that. God, how I wish you were here Daddy! Where are you? Some day I will find you and I will play for you.

Meanwhile Willie and Fontaine continued to fight and I no longer had my brother Jessie to talk to. I had never felt so alone, so abandoned and violated, I turned to the only thing in the world I could trust any more.....my piano.....my savior!

Chapter 3

I was becoming a woman; I was no longer the sweet little Jacqui at the piano in the pinafore and patten leather shoes. Attitudes toward me were changing and I will never forget the crushing horror of how I was treated when I started to menstruate. Mother never looked at it as a normal human function of eliminating waste; to her it was the terrible realization of the fact that I was able to bear children. For some reason I was a nasty, dirty person because I had started to bleed. I remember a story Mother told about Birdell, about how she reacted when she started her period; she would go down to the creek and wash herself, trying to make it go away. I had to learn about it on my own. I just can't imagine the primitive ignorance and the fear. How horrible!

To make matters worse I cycled too often; between nineteen and twenty one days, so she took me to the doctor thinking my thyroid was out of kilter and all he said was, "That's just her, leave it alone, don't mess with it." I was regular, though, and we used to wear pads, which I hated because I couldn't go out and play with the boys and girls of the neighborhood. I always preferred to play with the boys probably because I was never really allowed to. I had to sit on the steps and just watch everyone go by. All the boys knew I had my period; what we called "the curse." In those days I had to put all my underclothes in the laundry tub and wash them with bleach. Willie couldn't bear any evidence of a perfectly normal female function. I guess it all goes back to ancient times when women were considered dirty, unclean and unfit; unfit certainly to sleep with. But I'll tell you, there was no more sitting on Fontaine's lap, no more football games on Sunday afternoon. I was no longer the little girl, Jacqui, and Mother had set the boundaries in concrete. Not that he ever tried anything; it had simply become a different world and I knew the rules; mainly not to bring any babies home from up the street or anywhere else for that matter.

There was a time when I fell in love with the boy next door. I was in love with Norman, the boy who lived across the street. I could look into Norman's bedroom and he into mine. I was on the third floor and he was on the second floor of a typical Boston brownstone. I would look down and we would moon and spoon at long distance. At the time it was the most wonderful thing in the world. But poor Norman, God bless him, I think he was one of my first loves and after all I didn't have Jessie any more but Jessie was my brother anyway, not a boy-girl love interest. And as for Edward, I only saw him on Wednesday evenings at the Armory. He also lived way across town in Roxbury. So Norman and I held this long distance love affair because I wasn't allowed to spend time with him or any other boy. The most Norman could do was walk with me home from school holding hands until we were too close to home and then it was apart because if a neighbor would see us, Willie would know in a heartbeat and all hell would break loose. But I would sit on the stairs and he would be across the street and it was such a wonderful feeling that someone was paying attention to me. But getting together wasn't tolerated, not at all, because you see, I was fertile; I was producible. So Norman and I would flirt long distance in the windows at various times of day in various stages of attire. We would blow kisses to each other and sign love messages in the air. But, oh my God, if Mother walked into my room, I would quickly pretend I was doing something else. She would yell, "What are you doing? You in that goddamn window again looking at that boy across the street?" And I would proceed to catch a tongue lashing you wouldn't believe.

I would wait for her to leave and then I would pull out some music that was soft and had a love theme. I would go to the piano and start playing as if Norman was standing right there listening and I would play as if I wanted him to love me and in time, in my mind, he did love me. I could feel it through the music. I could almost feel him through the music. The next day I couldn't wait to see Norman, and hold his hand, and walk home from school, and he didn't even know how I had played for him.

Despite all the terrible problems growing up in my home, I will forever be grateful for mother and my aunts' insistence on education. They knew it was the way to a better life; a life that had been denied to them simply because of the accident of their birth. It gave me the opportunity to follow my passion, my piano. I was so lucky because the history of young blacks moving north to the Promised Land was that they were, for the most part, denied education of any significance. It was difficult at best for adult blacks to get decent work let alone send their children to good schools. White America was in great need of labor but preferred the influx of Eastern Europeans and the Irish flocking to the industrial centers of our country; Boston included. Therefore industry had the pick of destitute people; preferring white adults, then white teenagers, then black female adults, then black male adults and finally black teenagers. Cheap labor in all instances; better than the south but still bare subsistence. This, again, points out the plight of the American Negro and what they had to overcome. I was truly the exception as my family sacrificed and labored in my behalf. It would be much later that I would learn to appreciate this fact.

I went to the Girls High School of Boston, which, I believe, was the only public high school for girls in the country at that time. Mother had sent me there because it was an all girls' high school trying desperately to avoid my contact with boys to the best of her ability. Here again I didn't have a lot of girl friends and dating boys was out of the question. I was kind of a loner but all the friends I did have were all white and/or European. I learned a great deal from these young people and I think it opened up my eyes to the rest of the world and the people it produced. I was quite happy at school and I was able to seriously dedicate myself to my piano. While in my junior year, I auditioned for and was accepted on scholarship to the Boston Conservatory of Music as a Special Student where I would attend on an after-school basis. I know now that in order to have been accepted I had to have had excellent grades as well as the piano talent. I was thrilled and I know that this opportunity started me thinking in terms of a life long passion of professional achievement. I also found out quickly that my prior music teacher had led me unforgivably in the wrong directions and I had a great deal to overcome. I had lost valuable time.

My Instructor at the Conservatory was Professor Georg Fior, a small, diminutive man who looked like death warmed over but who demanded and stretched me and my skills better than anyone before. He demanded preparation and sometimes I was far from being so. There were times that I hadn't worked hard enough or long enough and my prior training was showing up. He would walk quietly up and down the stage smoking his cigarette, holding it between his index finger and thumb, with his elbow on his other hand in a very European manner. I remember seeing Claude Rains smoke that way in the movies and I always thought it was really sexy. He may have been quiet but he would quickly have me in abject tears within minutes because of my lack of preparedness. It was then I knew my work was cut out for me.

I graduated from high school after four years with honors and received high achievement awards. I was quite proud of myself but I was now finding that that sort of achievement wasn't as well accepted by the black community, including my mother Willie. Someone like me was considered to be "too good for the rest of us" and I'm not so sure she really meant, "too white." As a result I started to lean away from my people to the extent that all of my relationships were associated with classical music. I was learning that the values expressed by other people; black, white, foreign or whomever, were many times very interesting and acceptable to me and they were more and more accepting of me for my philosophies and values. I was growing up and it was getting more difficult at home as a result.

The Boston Conservatory of Music accepted me as a full time student in the fall after graduation from Girls High. I received a good scholarship and I was ecstatic because I would now be able to study with the best talent that Boston could produce. I was full time music now and the challenges became intense. My studies under Georg Fiore continued and I was consumed with what he required as with the other professors who expanded my scope of the music experience. Yes, there was a great deal to overcome. So what else was new?

I worked very, very hard at the Conservatory. Mother scrubbed floors until her knees were bloody and she did everything she could in those days to pay my expenses. She and James actually bought me an upright piano, my piano! I don't even know where they found her but I couldn't keep my hands off of her. She was made of that deep purplish mahogany and the surface showed the signs of use, but loving use. She wasn't new but it was heavy and had a tremendously fine soundboard. My piano was well balanced and voiced very well. I loved the rumbling bass and the bright treble and as I played, she would resonate throughout my body. She was beautiful and no one could touch her and I treated her like the member of the family she was. We put her in a little anteroom off the hall and that is where I lived with her whenever I could. Fontaine was not allowed to smoke in that room and nobody could clean and caress her but me.

We had moved to Symphony Road in the Back Bay right behind Symphony Hall. I was within walking distance of the Conservatory, which is right off The Fenway and also near Symphony Hall. Consequently I was very active at school. I would stay after school and practice until my fingers were numb. I would have loved to live in the dormitories but black people weren't allowed in those days. I did a great deal of accompanying, much of which was with the Chamber Music groups and I loved it. I was starting to realize my talent and with the marvelous instruction I was receiving, my confidence was increasing to new levels. I wanted all I could get and seized upon every opportunity to improve my skills. For the first time I was becoming aware of other people. I even admired many of them because we were all there for the same reason, doing what I was doing. It was a little like a coming home.

I still enjoyed going to the Armory with Fontaine on those Wednesday nights when I could break away from my studies. I always liked to see Edward, he wasn't the average black boy. He had the same class as his father. He spoke beautiful English and had a warm, friendly personality that made his smile make sense. He was of light brown skin as was his father because they were of Cuban ancestry and I was enormously attracted to him. Edward had a good job and had his own car and we started going out together but not exactly with the blessings of either mother. Fontaine was supportive of me and Edward but his father was too involved in his career to be concerned with two adolescents and their interest in each other. If Willie had known about our involvement, she would have done everything in her power to bring the relationship to a screeching halt. Consequently we had to sneak around behind her back. Everything had to be done under cover with lies, deception and guilt.

Edward gave me the wonderful support of my music that I so craved. Fontaine never came to my concerts, he just didn't understand. Mother came to a few but almost as an obligation. I now had that someone to bring into my life; into my relationship with my piano; someone who could love us both. My love affair was now a triangle, a threesome. We began to date but most of it was secretively, almost a cloak and dagger type of contact. Our parents knew that we were interested in each other but his parents and certainly Willie would not allow us to be in a situation where we could be intimate with one another. Intimate?! Holy shit were we intimate! I discovered sex with this wonderful, gentle, loving man and it was everything I had ever dreamt it would be, but more. It started sotto voce, a soft, caressing, exploring of each other's body while sharing the whispered words that began the slow, seductive, undulating press against each other. We became one and we were entwined in the rapid movement of passion as, for the first time, I felt the same oneness, the same simultaneous giving and taking that I had known from my piano. We moved faster and faster, allegro (con moto) with gradual crescendo to finale. Oh my God, the finale, the sforzando, was an experience rivaling birth itself. Every instrument in my soul was playing at once to the maximum of its humanness. Sated and complete, we laid next to each other in the bed of our new existence and the quiet of our breathing replaced any words we might have had for each other. We knew we were here for each other.

We knew it was real and now we had to find out, in the spring of our youth, what were we to do with it.

In the months and year that followed, Edward and I saw each other at every available moment. Willie knew that there was something going on but she had her hands full with Fontaine and with work and keeping her home together, we were able to avoid her quite easily. Edward would come to see me after his work and when I was playing in recital or in concert he was always there to bolster my self-critique, to flatter my sense of self. I would see him in the wings of the stage waiting for me to exit and the smile on his face told me everything I needed to know about my performance. Edward was my friend and lover and even though we were only twenty years old, we had to figure out how to make this wonderful togetherness permanent.

There was no way we could get married in Massachusetts without parental consent and the image of Willie and Edward's parents affixing their names to a consent form was nothing short of hilarious. Edward told me that we could get married in New Hampshire without consent but we had to go and get our blood tests two weeks before a marriage was possible. We decided, we went, we did it. Two weeks later, on the big day, Edward picked me up in front of the local Rexall drug store and we drove to Salem, New Hampshire. I, the nervous bride, so to speak, wore my usual attire of dungarees and an untucked shirt. The handsome, svelte groom wore slacks and a sport shirt, both of which could have used some ironing. No flowers, no pictures, no limousine, no bridesmaids, no groomsmen, no maid of honor, no best man; just Edward and me, this little Justice of the Peace, and a witness who was some relative of the JP who was clearly bored to tears. The JP was this little lady with flowing white hair and a big smile who obviously had performed hundreds of clandestine marriages of young people who were running from restraint. The whole, magnanimous event took about twelve and a half minutes, after which we jumped back into the car, drove back to the Rexall drugstore where Edward dropped me off. I went back to school, he went back to work and we tried desperately to pretend that it was just another day when we went home.

We knew we had to let our parents know that we had wed. The specter of telling Willie that I had done something like this without her knowledge was something like confronting Jack the Ripper in a dark alley. I made sure that Fontaine was going to be there. He had always been the buffer between Mother and me when she was going to get violent. So Edward and I approached the seated Willie and told her we had something to tell her. I saw the muscles in her jaw working and her already thin lips became a straight thin line. Her hands fidgeted with the buttons on her smock.

Daddy stood by the bedroom doorway. "Mother, Edward and I got married," I blurted. The statement sank in. I could see that split second moment of realization of what was said and the immediate translation into anger.

"You what?" she screamed. And I mean screamed. This scream is still reverberating in City Hall. She stood and started to walk toward us, I was scared shitless, Edward was catatonic, riveted to the floor and it was Fontaine who stepped between us, saving us from the onslaught of Mount Vesuvius in eruption.

"W-W-Willie, they are not children anymore. They can d-d-d-do what they th-th-th-think is right. Don't you give them shit," Fontaine stuttered with more confidence and conviction than I had ever seen him use with Mother. She stopped in her tracks, she was stunned, she looked at James and then at us, and much to my abject surprise, she cried. This is the first time I had ever come up a winner in a confrontation with my mother and certainly one of the first times I had ever seen her cry. My emotions were running wild, I was in love, I was afraid and now I was triumphant in confrontation with mother. We left her apartment and my knees were jelly.

Now it was Edward's turn to tell his parents. He preferred that I not be there so he went alone. It was not easy for Edward to tell the Colonel, the lawyer, the Superior Court Justice, the graduate of Harvard Law School, the 1932 Olympics track team member and well-known public figure that his son had just married this black piano student from Boston. A girl who had come from virtually nothing. Not to mention the response from his social climbing, Cuban mother who never had liked the fact that we were dating to begin with. She was convinced that our marriage was nothing more than an inconvenience that could be resolved by annulment.

The Colonel reacted with his expected signature aloofness as though a fly had just landed on his glass of scotch. Edward told them there would be no annulment and that we had found our own place to live and packed up his belongings and moved out.

I moved out of mother's soon after and Edward and I moved into our sweet little apartment in Roxbury. The apartment was a first floor, one bedroom, clean and cozy love nest in a very nice neighborhood. We were happy and comfortable. Edward would drop me off at school each day on his way to work and I resumed my studies while staying to practice after school. We were progressing nicely, my life had gained a sense of order. I plunged back into the routine of school and I was rapidly approaching graduation.

However in addition to my flaming love affair and marriage to Edward and being engrossed in my studies I had another interesting and almost life altering experience. Everything seemed to be happening at once when I met the French Language Instructor at the

Conservatory, Susan Roslindale. She took an immediate liking to me and I to her. Every other day I would go to her house after school and from the moment I entered the door I was to speak nothing but French. We read newspapers, the Reader's Digest and my piano lessons. We talked about Edward, family, the future and just about anything that was of interest at the moment, but it had to be in French, only French. And I love the French language. I'm sure that at some time in a prior life, I lived there and spoke it fluently. I love to say the words out loud and people hear me, even today, thinking I'm somewhat of a ham and that of course is true, I am.

Susan told me that the natural progression for me, as with other serious students of the piano, was to obtain a Fullbright Scholarship and go to Europe to study. I applied immediately but found that I was too late. Susan then suggested that we try for a French government fellowship. My application went in that day and I waited anxiously for weeks for word from Paris. One of the most joyous days of my life was when I went to the mailbox and saw the letter from the Gouverment Francais and with shaking fingers tore the envelope apart. I was accepted subject to proof of transportation to and from Paris. Again, Susan came to my rescue and we applied again to the Fullbright Foundation for travel funds. I was amazed when we were accepted within a week.

Edward and I were home one day when his mother, Amelia, virtually flowed into the room wearing a floor length mink coat. There are mink coats to the knee; there are mink jackets; there are mink stoles but this was a full, floor length mink coat. This Cuban, social elitist had made her entrance as if on stage. She looked at me with all the hatred that was in her and asked, "Well, are you pregnant?"

"No", I responded with all the humor that was in me.

FULLBRIGHT FELLOWSHIP WINNER

"Why then, are you going to Europe," she retorted as angry as before. And that is when my anger surfaced. I told her that this was an opportunity of a lifetime. Something I had worked all my life to accomplish and nothing, nothing was going to stand in my way from going to Paris. Amelia turned on her heel and huffed out of the room like a dust devil almost catching her floor length mink coat in the slamming door.

I turned to Edward and he said nothing. I wondered why.

Chapter 4

Edward and I were married but like many young people with their juices flowing, we got married for the wrong reasons. In our day sex was not allowed unless we were married. We were good friends and got along well but the main bonding of the relationship was sex. And, oh God, was it wonderful! I had never known anything like it in my life. He had a very strong sex drive and was not afraid to try new things to satisfy me. He was a wonderful lover and very kind and tender to me. I was never afraid or in pain and when he looked at me, I knew he wanted me and I was equal to his desire.

Edward Gourdin, Jr. was a very nice looking young man, rather short and slender with nice shoulders. He had been a sprinter on the track team at school and had the lithe body of a runner. He was a mechanic by trade and had taken shop classes in school and excelled in his trade. This was good money for us in those days and Edward paid the bills. I, of course, had my scholarship for school and there is no doubt that his mother gave him whatever he needed, whenever he needed it; a problem we would face later on. All in all I was very happy at this time of our lives and we had developed a nice circle of friends who would stop by and socialize over a few drinks and take-out chicken. These were Edward's friends as I had no real friends of my own because of my piano. My piano was all I had as mine and it was enough.

Our marriage was a result of my running away from my mother, Willie, and he, Edward, was running away from his father, Edward the senior. My Edward had spent his life trying to gain his father's love and respect to no avail. His father was a straight-backed Colonel in the Army Reserves, an attorney and judge while his son had achieved far less as a mechanic and high school dropout, all of which resulted in a dysfunctional relationship. The disparity between expectations and reality were too much for either to cope with. His father was a military man with a military mind but he had a kind heart and a strong compassion for the human condition, and despite his relationship with Edward, he was, for me, another father figure. I loved him with all my heart and he made me feel so special whenever he spoke with me. He treated me with all the affection I never had at home. Maybe it was an educational thing but he gave me the love and tenderness that Fontaine simply could not do. I remember him taking me out in the back yard and showing me how to swing a golf club telling me I was a natural. Nobody had ever told me before I was a natural anything. He would make himself his ever-present scotch and water and sit with his legs crossed and talk with me about things that were important to me, mainly my piano. He was wonderful and I respected him immensely. With all his warmth he was also a stately, stoic man who could dismiss you with a look if there was reason to do so. It was this demeanor that, combined with his Harvard law degree, cum laude, that resulted in his appointment as a civil court judge. He consciously chose civil law because he had a natural ability to settle disputes but could never be involved or certainly be responsible for sending someone to prison. It just wasn't in him.

Amelia, Edward's mother was a different story. She was a small, slender woman of Cuban descent with a very fair complexion. What she spent on clothes and jewelry each month would have paid our rent. Her resentment of me was very apparent to me and everyone around her. She condescended the best she could but condescension was the best emotion she could muster as I had taken her baby boy from her. I was the girl from across the tracks and was of no account. Her dislike for me was not just societal, it was ethnic and racial. This was spawned by her Cuban cultural background which held great disdain for blacks. In the Caribbean mindset, there are blacks and there are blacks. There are those with African features and characteristics and those of European ancestry. The Gourdin family was of the later variety; very fair of skin and straight hair while my heritage was from black slaves. Consequently, Amelia looked down her nose at me as a second-class citizen She showed no interest and couldn't care less about my music ability or what I meant to her son. She ignored the fact that her husband enjoyed my company and would spend such meaningful time with me. I was a non-entity in her eyes and I was totally uncomfortable in her presence. As a result, Edward tried to protect me as much as possible because he felt the same uncomfortableness as did I. However, Edward had to maintain his relationship with his mother and there was no way I would ever come between the mama bear and her cub. Besides the mother-son relationship there was a financial tie that he could never allow to be broken. He needed her financial support whenever he needed it and she was perfectly willing to give it on demand. I was an outsider who gave him the sex we both needed and loved but I was never allowed to be a true wife to him. I would never be a part of the family equation.

The symptoms of this toxic relationship were seeping to the surface as I prepared to go Europe. I don't think anyone thought I could or would accomplish the dream that I had dreamt for so many years. All of a sudden I was the woman who was going to abandon her husband. As a result of these utterly failing relationships, the reality of my decision materialized and I went about the process of graduation and departure. Paradoxically, my mother emerged in support of my move since it got me away from Edward. Willie had never come to visit me after our marriage, she had been so opposed to it but Fontaine did on occasion as he was still a part of the Wednesday night Armory Guard and still in such awe of Edward's father. Mother was still working for the Jewish families and provided me with the hand-me-down clothes from the girls in the families. These were top-of-the-line clothes, not the Good Will variety. These were stylish outfits with white gloves and feathered hats with dresses that showed off my womanliness. My wardrobe was becoming complete and I was ready to board the Queen Elizabeth bound from New York to Southampton.

The trip to New York was a quiet exercise in wonderment and disbelief. My mother had virtually disappeared from my life since I had married the year before and now here she was-sitting beside me on the train-to put me on the boat-to go to Europe-to study piano-which she had never understood or fully appreciated. I can only surmise that she had told people about it and had gotten some positive responses and congratulations that her daughter could have achieved so much. Maybe her ego had been stroked by the attention but all of a sudden she wanted to be a part of it and I may never understand why. Beyond all this I was so excited I couldn't sit still. This was actually happening to me and I was afraid someone would pinch me and I would wake up from my Cinderella dream. I thought the train ride would never end but here was New York and of all people to greet us but Aunt Hazel. We spent the night at Hazel's and in the morning we walked up the long ramp to the Queen Elizabeth, the flagship of the Cunard Line. My ticket said that my stateroom was on the "D" Deck and after making inquiries I found myself in the bilge of the boat below the water line in a room not more than five by eight with bunk beds and a washbowl and nothing more. "D" Deck now we laughingly called "Dungeon Deck." Not too elegant but I didn't care. That is where all the students were housed and I was on my way.

It was truly amazing that I was on my way. Rosa Parks, a work weary woman had stubbornly kept her seat when told to relinquish it to a white person just two years before. Just one year before the Montgomery Improvement Association was forming to boycott Montgomery's bus system causing nothing but grief for the whites dependent on black domestic help to wash their clothes and dishes. Martin Luther King, Jr. was becoming prominent in the non-violent war on segregation and bigotry. The voices of the civil rights movement were becoming loud and clear but I must say that I was immune from these issues. They were not a part of my life in Massachusetts other than not being allowed to stay in the Conservatory dormitories. Willie and her sisters would talk about it but there was no direct impact on my life at that time. I was so naïve regarding political things; things that were happening primarily in the south. I was a musician and all I was interested in was my piano and the ability to improve my skills. I would find myself, later on, defending this wonderful country of ours, with all of its racial faults. I was the musician who happened to be black, not the black who happened to be able to play the piano.

My roommate was a mousy little girl named Patty. She was tiny and pale with mouse-brown hair and about as nondescript as the wall. She was very nice and wanted to know all about me and we talked for a long time about how we got where we were. She was heading for the Sorbonne where she was to major in academics which fit her entire persona perfectly. She had never been away from home and certainly not in a foreign country and I hadn't either. She was scared to death, which I was not, so she clung to me like a magnet on the fridge. She was not only petrified about the boat passage but she was continually seasick. There was nothing she could eat and keep down and I couldn't get away from her. So every time she got sick, the crew would clean up and give me apples and saltines to force her to eat something. This I was reluctant to do as she would just lose them within minutes. Poor Patty.

Out to sea I became more and more familiar with the boat and could get around without getting lost. Patty was doing better and we had been assigned to a certain table for meals. This is where the magic began. There were two men at that table who were to become major players in the unfolding events of my life. Two young men who would not only help shape my destiny but I theirs as well.

I was attractive and dressed to the nines and Lawrence Phillips and Jean Francois Chivot were two gorgeous males and delightful company. We shared our stories and dreams for the future and laughed through every meal. Lawrence, or Laurie as he preferred to be called, was a very tall man with a very thick British accent and equally thick eyeglasses who loved to laugh and tell jokes, and he was good at it. Jean Francois, to the contrary, was handsome but quite short and more laid back and pensive but he knew just what to say to top the entire conversation. The food was marvelous with just the right wines selected by our french friend and the evening meal went well into the night. I flirted continually with them both and I could sense the slight competition for my attention, and I loved every minute of it. The elegance of the evening was what I had only read about before and now here I was, Jacqui Gourdin, the girl of the piano, submersed in a cosmopolitan ambiance that Roxbury would never know.

This romance of the sea lasted five days and we had many activities on the boat that I and my shadow, Patty, enjoyed to the fullest. I felt alive and well, everything agreed with me and at the end of each day I luxuriated in our dinners together. Our relationships became deeper and deeper as the nuances of our lives became known. Jean Francois promised me that once I was settled at the Cite, our school campus, he would show me Paris and I told him I would be delighted if he did. Laurie invited me to England to introduce me to the grandeur of London and I wanted to see that too, and I told him so. These were becoming dear friends and I knew the friendships would not disappear at the Southampton dock. Oddly enough I realized that I had not thought about Edward once in five days.

The QE docked at Southampton on schedule where Laurie hugged his goodbyes and headed for his ground transportation to London. Jean Francois, Patty and I were shuttled off to clear customs and board the Boat Train crossing the Channel to Paris. Paris! I was mesmerized, it was everything I had ever seen in the movies or read in books or was told it was. "The City of Lights," was to become my City of Lights; it was to become the light of my life where I could finally consummate my lifelong passion for the piano. This was the land of the grand masters, this was the land of learning, of romance, of antiquity, and I was going to be part of it. I had come alive and little Jacqueline Jones, the girl in the pinafore and patten leather shoes seemed generations ago.

Chapter 5

The bus pulled up to the boat terminal and I was told it was my bus taking me to my new home at the Cite. The streets were full of cars and people going in every direction. These were little tiny cars with high pitched horns and people had to jump out of their way because there was no way they were going to stop. It was a cacophony of sound as I jumped onto the bus and my heart was racing so fast I was light headed. I sat in my seat and pressed my nose against the window like a third grader at a pet store window. Everyone around me was talking in French. Not the French I had studied! I thought I was going to understand and speak like a local but this was a brand of French I had never heard before and it was all around me. Not just one or two people speaking slowly but the whole goddamn bus was talking at once and I didn't understand a word. So I pressed my nose against the window again, shut out the sounds and just looked. The bus ride took some time and I was able to absorb the diverse appearances of many neighborhoods. I wanted to take it all in at once but it was too much, I was flabbergasted and I finally just sat and tried to put my numbed arms around the fact that I was in Paris.

The bus bumped and thumped to a stop and the driver announced in French that we had arrived at the Cite. I scrambled down the steps and looked for the first time at the place where I would be spending the next nine months of my life. Le Fondation Des Etats-Unis was the living quarters for American students and I found, as I looked around, that there had been about ten other students who were obviously Americans like me. I would find later that they were French majors and spoke the language a hell of a lot better than I did. The front door was right on the Boulevard and we, along with our luggage, entered a large lobby with marble floors, enormously high ceilings and carved mahogany doors at least seven feet in height with alabaster door knobs. But the curving marble stairway with dark red carpeting took my breath away. This stairway would make 'Gone With The Wind' look drab. The steps at the top were wide but as the staircase cascaded down to the main floor, the size of the stairs increased in width. It was a glacier of red and white flowing in a graceful arch. The bottom stair had to be thirty feet across. A stairway to die for! I was in awe of everything around me. All of the furniture, the large reception desk and wall fixtures were massive and heavy looking. It had a museum quality, not ornate but overwhelmingly impressive.

A very pleasant woman introduced herself to us as the resident housemother and announced that we were to fill out some forms, which included all the vital information needed to manage us as students in her care. This took some time after which we were shown to our rooms, restrooms, cafeteria and study halls. The rooms I was primarily interested in were the piano rooms, which were conveniently located two floors above my floor, which made it easily accessible. But I also loved my dorm room; a room for two students. The bed was comfortable and the room was of good size with plenty of closet space, which I needed considering the enormous quantity of clothes I had brought to France. There were two study desks with chairs and a chest of drawers for each. The tall, ten-paned French windows opened outward and we overlooked the campus green lawn below. It was warm and comfortable and now all it needed was another person.

I had gotten settled in my new home for two days when I was told that I was going to meet my roommate. I was flopped on my bed contemplating all that had happened thus far when I heard the key in the door. I jumped to my feet just as the door swung open and there stood a tall, statuesque and somewhat mysterious looking girl about my age who looked at me momentarily and said, "Jacqui?" Her french accent made it sound like "Jockey?"

"You must be Laure," I said with a smile reaching for her hand.

"Yes I am Laure, Laure Valay," she answered in very broken English. Laure sat down facing me on the twin beds and we started a conversation that was to be the beginning of an instantaneously close and wonderful relationship. She was not a beautiful woman in the American sense but she was very tall and had chiseled features that bordered on pretty with thick, shiny brown hair to her shoulders. We talked for hours, she struggling with English and I with French. But through all our bumbling and groping for the words we were able to understand each other perfectly. That could only come from people who liked each other instantly, who could read all the languages of the body and see your soul through your eyes. We accomplished in a few hours what it took others the whole school year, if at all. As we talked, I gushed out my whole life story and as I did, bit-by-bit her mysteriousness disappeared and she became as open as I. I told her about my black, southern upbringing, about my mother and aunts, about Edward and his father. But most of all I told her about my piano and what the piano meant to me and what it had meant to me for most of my life. She suddenly came out of that reserved, mysterious mannerism and looked me right in the eye as she told me of her family, her loves, her fears, her failures, her hopes and desires and how she loved children and wanted to be a teacher more than anything in the world. She told me of a simple and quiet childhood in southern France. Her father and mother were merchants and although not rich they knew the value of education and had given her the best that the region could provide. Laure had excelled, and, like me, had received a scholarship to the Sorbonne, the best that France had to offer. She was here to become the best teacher she could so that she could return to Avignon and instruct the children of her little town, but she also wanted to know Paris and the excitement of Paris. We decided that we were both going to enjoy the excitement of Paris no matter what. We also made a pact that on certain days of the week we would only speak in French and on others, only English. She needed to learn English and I needed French; it was perfect. When our conversation became exhausted we realized how close we had become. I felt like I had known her all my life; we felt like sisters.

Sisters yes, but in contrast to me, Laure's wardrobe was less than half of mine. If I had twelve of something, she had four. Four pair of underwear, four blouses, four skirts, two pair of shoes. "You Americans," she would tease, "why do you need all that?" To which I answered by telling her of the over-abundance of choices in America. Things don't have to last as long because they are so relatively cheap. "How fortunate you all are," she observed and she was right.

The next few days were spent practicing and honing my piano skills as I would soon register for my instruction and when I did, I would have to give my instructor an example of my skills. This would be a form of audition in that my professor would determine whether I met the standards of L'Ecole Normale or not, and if not I would lose my government fellowship and they would send me home. That would be a devastating event I could never let happen. It would be the end.

Upon registering I found that I would not be in a classroom setting but rather traveling to the studio of my professor, Jules Gentil. I had to learn to get from the Cite to his residence and that would be by subway called Metro, which was a most frightening experience. They had written directions for me and explained everything thoroughly but when I descended to the station among the milling throng of people, my confidence vanished, I was afraid and couldn't remember a word of French or what I was to do. It was a harrowing trip I'll never forget. Only God knows how it happened but I found myself on the right train going in the right direction and got off at the right station within blocks of Gentil's residence. At twenty-two years of age, in a foreign country and having just come all the way across the city by myself, I had a return of confidence that took me by surprise. I felt like I had just climbed Everest and I knew I would pass my audition. I knew he would like me, not just my piano skill but all of me. I would meet his standards on every level; piano, character, perseverance and most of all, desire. I almost ran to his studio.

I double checked the directions and found his residence and studio easily. His apartment building was several stories of typical French concrete with manicured hedges along the sidewalks. I climbed the stairs quickly and rang the floor for the elevator. The apartment door opened and to my surprise a small woman was standing there smiling kindly. I introduced myself to Madame Gentil and she responded in a very soft voice with perfect American English that she knew who I was. She ushered me to the front room, which had many windows overlooking the city, and in the center of the sparsely appointed studio was a large grand piano, behind which stood a man. He was rather short and rotund, balding with a wonderfully round face and dancing blue eyes. Monsieur Gentil smiled at me and I at him as we extended the formal handshake. I liked him immediately but I had to tell him what was burning in my mind. I had to tell him to speak slowly if I were to understand his instruction and when I did, he laughed, he really laughed out loud. Suddenly I realized this was as new to him as it was to me. He had never had a black American student before, especially one who was so outspoken without the normal French social correctness. Normally the professor spoke and the student listened, that was the European way, but here was a little black girl from America who within five minutes had respectfully told the professor what he had to do. It struck him funny and we got along famously from then on. He liked my spirit and spunk and at that moment the realization hit me that Jacqui had done it, she was here, the dream was unfolding and her professional career had just begun.

He asked me for my repertoire and background as to how long I had been playing, where I had studied, who my instructors had been and what was I prepared to play for him. The language was returning and I did well, mistakes and all, without help from Madame Gentil and I was comfortable with my ability to communicate. My fear was gone, all the emotion of the day subsided and in the comfort zone of his studio I played for him and played as well as I ever had.

Professor Gentil paused for a long moment when I finished and without praise, thanked me and as he pointed out those aspects of my performance he liked and those that needed work I could feel the enormity of his experience and his tremendous powers of observation. From these observations he immediately outlined the nature of my studies and where I was to place the emphasis in practice. I realized I had been given an extraordinary teacher, I was blessed, and as I rode home on the Metro I vowed I would give my piano every fiber of my being and I would give Monsieur Gentil all the respect he deserved. He had accepted me on face value and I would dedicate myself to the fact that his decision was not only a good one, but a great one. And I'll be damned; I got off at the right station.

Paris, for me, at that time, and considering my decision to dedicate my heart and soul to my piano, could have been Hoboken, New Jersey as far as I was concerned. The city meant nothing. The only thing that mattered was my education and proficiency at the piano. My normal day consisted of getting up, getting ready and eating a mini breakfast on the fly as I flew out the door to L'Ecole Normale for a day of classes. There would be fifteen or more students in the class, all speaking French, and Monsieur Gentil conducting the class in French as well. I would seat myself next to an English speaking person who was fluent in French so I could get help when necessary. Everyone was helping everyone, no one minded helping another. It was a wonderfully nurturing environment and I was quite comfortable.

Monsieur had a unique and interesting method of teaching. Each student was assigned a certain part of a piece and each day one of us would be asked to play that assignment. He would then begin to pick it apart, explaining as he went what should have been done and, at times, actually playing what he was talking about. Those blue eyes of his would sparkle like sapphire gemstones and when a student excelled he would respond with a joyous fist clenched, raising his arms as though he was watching his soccer team make a goal. "That is it," he would shout, or, "She has it, that is good," and when it happened to you, you felt you had just won the Gold at the Olympics. But when things went wrong the sapphires dulled and all patience flew out the door as he couldn't understand why you didn't get it. There was no bullshitting Monsieur Gentil. I felt truly sorry for those who were not prepared for the day. The Maitre was truly the Master of the class and although he was a gentile man as his name signifies, his frustration was plainly evident when he sensed lack of dedication. He commanded such respect that it was rare that a student would deserve such treatment. The pressures of his classes were enormous and the students bonded closely, while collectively we tried to solve a given problem. We would meet after class and try to resolve the issues of a particular piece that were causing us difficulty. It was in this manner that we learned from each other and I was very grateful for my friends in class.

After class it was back to the Cite for lunch and off to the practice room. We all had assigned times where we could go to the practice room on the top floor. It was getting cold and the heating system was suspect so I would immediately try to warm my hands. The best way to do that was to play the piano with a relaxed vengeance. The next three to five hours were a daily opportunity to put into effect those things we had learned in

Just Me and My Piano

class. It was my world, this little room, just large enough for the piano and maybe an extra chair. No windows, no pictures, just lamps on the walls. It was just my piano and me and I was in my daily "chambre du joie."

I would not stop playing until my body was spent; actually drained of physical and mental energy. The smart part of me would say to stop but the belligerent, driven part of me wanted to stay there and get it. It was then, giving up, I would go to my room. I would meet Laure and tell her of my misery and she would listen to my tirade carefully with a well-intentioned, understanding look on her face and when she could break in on the conversation, she would simply say, "You need to eat, girl." So we would.

Many times we would just sit and talk. Her studies at the Sorbonne were demanding, and she had a great deal of paperwork every day and the workload was intense. We would talk about everything; life, love, studies and what it was like growing up in France and likewise in America. She was extremely comfortable to talk to and although I never had a sister, or brother for that matter, she was about as close to being a sibling as I could imagine. The French are not, on the whole, easy to talk to. They are more self-contained and don't open up like we Americans. They need to know who you are before they give of themselves. Laure, however, must have sensed my honesty and sincerity because she was as free to talk with me as I with her.

Laure and I had developed a clique of friends who would meet periodically in the downstairs foyer. We would drape ourselves over the overstuffed chairs and sofas and talk of the many topics of the day. Being the only black American in the group, I was continually tested and challenged based on the current headlines, which were largely in regard to the civil rights movement in the United States. We read about Little Rock, about Martin Luther King, Jr. and his non-violent rebellion. There were articles about the famed Rosa Parks whose protest actions started the whole movement into motion. My friends seized on these news reports and used them to criticize my country. I found myself defending our country from slavery all the way through emancipation, to the role of the modern black in modern society. I did the best I could but frankly I wasn't all that knowledgeable. The civil rights movement had never really been a part of my life. Of course I knew that things were going on and I read the papers like everyone else but segregation and bigotry had never really altered my world, my reality. The only thing that I had been denied because I was black was that I could not reside in the dormitories at the Boston Conservatory. The newspapers, however, were full of the violence in the big cities and all through the south, and my friends could not understand how I could love a country that treated minorities is such a manner. Finally, out of frustration and some anger, I finally told them to back off. I told them that there was no way I could have been where I was, doing what I was doing if I lived in any other country. I was unscathed by segregation and bigotry and I was as happy as anyone could be and simply because I had my piano, an excellent maitre and good friends. What else could a little black girl from Boston want in life? I was happy and I didn't want them telling me I shouldn't be! They backed off.

I was developing a good routine. My studies with Monsieur Gentil were a continuous part of my growing abilities on the piano and I would practice each day to exhaustion. I was growing, I was getting better and all thoughts of home and Edward were fewer and fewer. I was comfortable in my Paris existence but little did I know what was in store for me.

Whenever someone received a phone call at the Cite, the switchboard in the foyer would transfer the call to the proper floor. One day there was a knock at my door and someone said there was a call for me. I hurried down the hall in my nightgown and pressed the receiver to my ear and heard that wonderfully soft voice of Jean Francois. It took me by complete surprise. We had promised at the ferry landing to contact each other but months had gone by and with all there was in getting settled into my studies, I had forgotten. He too had had a great deal to do upon arrival as he was taking over his father's business in central France and consequently had not spent much time in Paris.

I was giddy, I was four feet off the ground and all my recollections of the Queen Elizabeth came roaring back bringing all the emotions with it. All I could do was run off at the mouth about all that had been happening here at the Cite and about my piano. I couldn't talk fast enough which made him laugh that little laugh he always gave me when he was amused. Jean Francois broke in by saying we would catch up on all that was happening when we got together, and that was to be that night. We would have dinner at one of his out-of-the-way restaurants. Not much in elegance but marvelous food and he had remembered how I loved jazz music. We were to go to a jazz club in Paris to complete the evening. That was Jean Francois' way. He would always have the evening or the day planned in advance and always with me and my interests in mind.

Jean Francois arrived at the Cite punctually at seven o'clock and I was as nervous as I had ever been. I remember that I wondered why. I wore a beautiful black suit with black, strapped high heels and as I descended that sweeping stairway, I felt as though I was in a play or a movie. It was elegance and I was part of it. Jean Francois stood at the bottom of the staircase so that he could see me descend and I could tell just from the look on his face that he approved. He showed his approval in only a way that Jean Francois could. His whole being showed his delight and I was ecstatic. I reached the foyer and went to him and we embraced. He was every bit as handsome as I had remembered from the boat and his manner just as gallant. He helped me with my coat and I signed out of the Cite and jumped into his Citroen parked at the curb.

My love, Jean Francois

The drive from the Cite to the restaurant was magic. All the lights of Paris were at my feet. The boulevards were busy with evening traffic as Jean Francois hurled his Citroen through the streets only as the French can do. He pointed out all the places of interest as we went and I realized how little of Paris I had seen since my arrival months before. The restaurant Veiux Navarre was off the main drag in a narrow side street. The Maitre d` obviously knew Jean Francois as he called him by name and welcomed me by offering the best table in the house. Jean Francois ordered our before dinner drinks and recommended the meal. He asked the Maitre d` to show us the meat before it was cooked to be sure it met his standard. It seemed as though the entire kitchen crew came out to receive his approval and I was amazed. I had never seen anything like this before and I was loving it.

The wine was perfect with dinner and we talked through the candlelight as we lingered over the elegant food. I told him of all that was happening to me and he listened with sincere interest. He then told me of the difficulty he was having taking over the operation of his father's manufacturing plant and all that it involved.

That was why I had not heard from him earlier and he apologized. We completed the dinner with the most wonderful cognac I had ever tasted and I had an opportunity to demonstrate my ability to hold my liquor. The same amount of alcohol with anyone else at any other time in any other place and I would have been blasted. We left the Veiux Navarre with warm words of thanks and with a grateful wait staff who had been obviously well rewarded. We walked to the car and I realized I had his arm in mine.

Le Club Jazz was across town in another narrow street part of the city. I was surprised to see a number of black Americans who were demonstrating their remarkable ability to be obnoxious. The French do not like the socially aggressive behavior they were demonstrating and I quickly let them know that I was there with a French gentleman and I was determined to abide by the rules that go with that relationship. Several asked me to dance during the evening and I politely refused as we just wanted to enjoy the music and intimately enjoy each other. My heaven that night was that tiny, dimly lit cabaret full of wonderful sounds and that smiling face across the table from me who entranced me with the flirtatious words of a man whom I would obviously see again.

We were more quiet on the way back to the Cite. The combination of the company, food, wine and the hour made me drowsy and pensive. I was warm inside and out and with my head against the window I gazed at Jean Francois as he drove me home. He would cast me a glance and I would smile. His smile back told me that he had enjoyed the evening as much as I. The Cite loomed ahead all too soon and Jean Francois discreetly parked away from the entrance. Without a word, he leaned over to me and we kissed. Not a passionate kiss but a warm and understanding kiss. A kiss I will never forget.

Chapter 6

If there was ever a love story, I was it. Jean Francois walked me to the Cite front desk as he always did, being the consummate gentleman he was. He wanted the desk clerk to actually see that I was brought home and brought home by him. He was always concerned for my person and especially because I was an American in his country.

I flew through the door to my room and there was Laure whose eyes grew quite large as she saw and heard her American roommate gush out the events of that wonderful evening. We talked for hours, she puffing relentlessly on her cigarettes, her Gaulois Cigarettes which were like Camels but twenty times as strong, so I smoked my own. I never smoked with Jean Francois because he didn't smoke at all but with Laure, we fogged the room.

This was a new chapter in my mission of coming to France. It was a beautiful departure from the tedium and stress of the piano. It was an instantaneous relationship and although we never had to say it, I knew he liked me very much and I knew I liked him equally and we never questioned that we wanted to be together. What made it even more exciting and enticing was that we couldn't see each other every day. We could only be together when he made his business trips to Paris. The situation left me perfectly free to study and practice without making allowances for someone else. But after one or two weeks with only phone calls, the anticipation of seeing Jean Francois was excruciating. I would virtually scream when they called to say the phone was for me. In this way I could commit myself totally to my piano and then to him when the time had come

During these first months I had not heard a word from Edward nor had I contacted him. I was perfectly content to ignore the fact that we were married. The reason was that we were never married in the literal sense. We had married for the wrong reasons and he was fulfilling his life in Dorchester each day and I was fulfilling mine in Paris. Marriage was a non-issue. I was in Paris for a reason and, really, nothing else mattered.....that is, except for Jean Francois.

We normally saw each other every two weeks when he made his trips to Paris from the factory. He would see his parents during the week, conduct business, then call me with plans for the weekend. When we were together I would tell him the things I wanted to do and the places I wanted to see and he would suggest things that I knew nothing about. Sometimes he would pick me up early in the day and we would travel to the various neighborhoods of Paris. Paris is like New York or Boston; New York with its Burroughs and Boston with its North End, Quincy, Dorchester, etc. We drove the Champs E'Lysee, we viewed the Arch De Triumph and the Eiffel Tower. Jean Francois would take me to the events I wanted to see, mostly symphonies and concerts of various kinds. He loved my clothes and I have never been without more clothes than I can wear. In Paris you don't just see something in the window you like and then pick it off the rack, you tell them what you want and they fit it for you. I would dress for Jean Francois and do my hair for Jean Francois, use perfume for Jean Francois and long for Jean Francois. He loved me for my Joie D' Vivre, my enjoyment of life. French women were much more reserved than I. I was all over the place with my enthusiasm and energy and he loved it. We truly, truly enjoyed each other's company and although we both knew it was going to happen, we had not had sex. Like everything else he did, it had to be right, not just a physical act but also a true expression between two people in love. It had to be almost planned and yet spontaneous at the same time. What happened before and after was as important as during. No one knows the Savoir Faire of love better than French men and among French men there was no one better than Jean Francois.

I finally had found a balance in my life. I was doing what I really wanted to do with my little dessert on the side. I wasn't totally tied to my piano, because if you do get totally caught up it can become a grind and when that happens, you are not as successful or happy. People think we're crazy to begin with. Anyone who can sit at a piano for five and six hours a day has to be a little unbalanced to say the least; Jean Francois was my balance.

I was learning a tremendous amount musically. We were kind of like a band of siblings at the Cite. We were all there for music and we had to struggle to learn the French way of conquering the piano. I was trying desperately to overcome the initial years of poor instruction. However, there were also social activities at the Cite that we all participated in without losing our individuality. We liked each other and worked together but were not dependent upon one another. You leave everything behind. The minute you enter that practice room everything else ceases to exist. After you have been there for a while, you actually achieve an altered state of consciousness. The concentration is so intense you become in between where you are, and where the music is taking you.

The weeks passed and my music was improving marvelously and so was my relationship with Jean Francois. I was approaching the same state of consciousness with him as I was with my piano. The stars were no longer in my eyes; I had to settle down. I was no longer the giddy, young American girl who had fallen in love in Paris and the seriousness of what was soon to happen matured our feelings for each other. The realization of what we both so eagerly wanted had dominated my every day but for the first time the remembrance of my being married re-entered my thoughts. No one had touched me since Edward and when the phone rang one day I knew that that was no longer going to be true. It was Jean Francois on the line and we chatted for a few moments and then he told me when he was going to pick me up and what I should be wearing and where we were going and that I should pack an overnight bag. The only thing he failed to mention was what we were going to be doing. After that phone call it was absolutely impossible to concentrate on anything. I was no good to myself or anyone else.

He picked me up at the Cite right on schedule and we drove to a small restaurant which was also a small hotel. The restaurant was on the first floor and the rooms were upstairs. It was similar to our bed and breakfasts in America but on a higher level, simply because it was French. We enjoyed a succulent meal which I barely remember as I was exceptionally nervous, which I tried desperately to hide and which was impossible to do.

After the meal, candlelight and cognac, we went to our room and the night of all nights began.

Jean Francois was a wonderful lover. He would start at the top and work his way down in a fashion that lit every fire in my mind and body. He was gentle and kind and understood my nervousness. His lovemaking was almost orchestrated with all the nuances of an adagio. Jean François seemed to enjoy my enjoying him as much as he was enjoying me. When we were complete I got out of bed and went to the french doors and stepped out onto a little balcony. It was cool and crisp and the moon was high. My robe wasn't enough and I shivered slightly. I turned to see Jean Francois looking at me from the bed and as I slipped my robe, I went next to him for more. It was a long and tender night, one which will live on in my memory forever.

The weeks became months and I fell into a beneficial routine that consisted of studies, friends at the Cite and, of course, Jean Francois. I had never been happier and things had a normalcy and a life flow that was at the same time, exciting and comforting. My friends, who were from several different countries, and I would go out occasionally for a drink at the local sidewalk cafe and we would continue learning about one another. Once again I was surprised with how much they knew about their countries in comparison to my knowledge of my own. We were a tight-knit group by now and had become known as the "boisterous ones" as our discussions many times became heated and very vocal. They still couldn't understand segregation in America. My problem was that I hadn't experienced it any more than they. I had truly been spared so my country was hard to defend except from my own limited experience. I didn't have the anger and frustration of the untold numbers of blacks who had been beaten, literally and figuratively, by the horrors of hatred and bigotry that had erupted back home.

Winter evaporated into spring and my time was dominated by preparing for exams. This was what it was all about and I concentrated as never before. The exams consisted of master classes whereupon Maitre Gentil and Monsieur Alfred Cortot, one of the greatest living pianists of the French school, would assess me. The entire class would also be present as well. Just imagine the magnitude of this culmination of everything I had worked for. My future, my piano, my life were hinged upon receiving a favorable assessment or it would all be over and I would be on my way home. A favorable assessment, however, would lead to my successful completion of my year in Paris and I would return with a certificate of merit that would make my future very bright. Did I work? Holy shit did I work!

Jean Francois was very understanding during this time and he backed off from making the normal demands on my time. He knew that I needed to be totally free to make an all-consuming effort to be successful. I missed him but I didn't really have time to miss him. He was calling frequently to encourage me and to help keep me focused on my work. He was there to boost my morale when I was down by telling me that I would be great and when he became serious like this he would speak nothing but French and I knew he was emphatically behind me. This was the kind of support I had never known before. He knew just what to say and I loved him all the more for it. The day had arrived and I was as fully prepared as I would ever be..........and scared to death.

Chapter 7

This was the day. This was the day that I had anticipated for what seemed all my life. The entire class assembled very early and we were abuzz with nervous chatter. We were all schoolgirls wearing skirts and sweaters and flats; typical college freshmen campus attire. We were new to the world of music and no one knew what Monsieur Cortot was like. Was he going to be super critical and heavy handed or was he more like Maitre, kind but direct?

Finally, after what seemed hours, Maitre Gentil and Monsieur Cortot entered the studio, walked briskly to the stage and stood before the piano. The entire class leaped to their feet immediately as if on cue. These were two of the most revered concert pianists in France, masters, and we were to play for them to determine whether we were competent enough to continue our studies. These were the Master Classes that determined whether we were able to concertize and handle the pressure, a pressure we knew we would be facing every time we set foot on the stage. This was a test of character as well as ability.

Monsieur Cortot was a short man like Maitre Gentil and to my delight he spoke beautiful English, which gave me a certain confidence. They started to call names and each student told the masters what piece they were to play and they were invited to start. Some did very well despite their nervousness but others were interrupted and gently brought back to the score with encouraging direction. These men were there to encourage and bring out success knowing the tremendous pressure each student was enduring. Those who were too nervous would probably not be able to concretize, or at least not at this time of their careers. The successful would add the Master Classes to their portfolios and go on to varying professional achievements.

My name was called and I took the longest walk of my young life; acknowledged the masters and announced that I was going to play a composition by Shuman. A powerful, uplifting and aggressively intense "Faschingsswank Aus Wien." I launched into this score with every fiber of my body and soul and within a few bars I was lost in my piano world of classical music. I was allowed to play the entire first movement without interruption, which gave me an immense lift of confidence. I completed the performance and the masters talked directly to me. The class could hear but they spoke only to me about my performance. They spoke to areas that might be improved by this technique or that. They suggested areas of study I should pursue to round out my abilities. They were objective and direct but the fact remained that they had not felt the need to interrupt and correct. That had happened to others but I was ecstatic that it hadn't to me. I smiled and thanked them and if I could have flown off the stage, I would have. One of my friends thought later that I had. I patiently waited for all to complete the class and virtually ran home to get Jean Francois' phone call and tell him of my wildly successful day. It was poor Laure who had to listen to it all until they told me there was a phone call for me.

When the dust had settled I sat down and wrote a long letter to my mother telling her of the successes I had had. She had been helping financially the entire year as she had for most of my educational years. Despite all the dysfunctional aspects of my upbringing; the anger, the fights, the alcohol and demonstrated dislike and condemnation of me, she had, for some strange reason always supported my musical efforts. She had paid for my early lessons and had provided the clothing obtained from the Jewish families and was now sending me money monthly to supplement my stipend. Although there were never words of affection, never hugs nor outward expressions of love or caring, for some reason there had been support in the only way she could; monetary support. For that reason, and that reason only, I owed her a letter of success.

My year at L'Ecole Normale ended with the Master Class and I now had to decide my future. I didn't want to leave. I had learned to love Paris, I certainly loved Jean Francois and my life was so complete I didn't want it to change. I went to him and we talked at great length and he wanted me to be sure that this is what I wanted and to prepare myself if it wasn't to be. I put my arms around his neck and looked into those blackish-darkish eyes and assured him that this is what I wanted and at that point all I wanted was…him.

The very next day I started the process that would lead to an extension of my fellowship. I had no idea if it was even possible but I was soon to find out. The American Embassy was among the throng of municipal buildings in the downtown area and I entered the typical cement block building, which had little character, if any. I told the receptionist what my mission was and she referred me to a very nice gentleman who, though French, spoke perfect English and asked me myriads of questions and recorded a great deal of information about me and my last year's activities. He explained that if this was to be approved there were several stipulations that had to be met. One, I could not work and earn money of any kind. Two, I had to study, and this included the summer months, which might be a problem. Professors normally do not teach in the summer months and most leave Paris for summer homes in other parts of France. In order for my fellowship to be extended I had to have a commitment from Monsieur Gentil that he would be willing to teach me during the summer season. And three, I had to make my own living arrangements considering I could not continue living at the Cite, and four, I could not leave the country.

Maitre Gentil smiled when I asked him if I could continue my studies another year. When Monsieur smiled at me, he smiled with his eyes. I was his crazy American, this flamboyant, black girl who had balls enough to go after what she wanted and worked like hell to get it, and he liked that. And I knew he liked me anyway; his eyes told me he liked me and I knew it from the start. He spent his summers in Annecy, a small French town on the border of Switzerland and he explained what was necessary to do to make it happen, and he made a point of telling me that this whole proposition was not normally done. I responded that I was fully prepared to meet these requirements and consequently he agreed to continue my instruction. He then surprised me by offering to help me find suitable living quarters in Annecy and suitable meant providing a piano. He knew the lady who rented rooms, and in France, rooms are not usually rented to foreigners unless there is a French person interceding for them. Monsieur Gentil was that person. I told him I was exceedingly grateful.

"Formidable," I shouted to Jean Francois who was as elated as I about my success with Monsieur Gentil and I went back to the Cite and finished my studies with the happy anticipation of a summer in beautiful Annecy and another year of continuing my fairy tale life with a second year of study and another year of Jean Francois.

Saying "goodbye" to my dear friends at the Cite was very difficult. My American friends were going back home and the others to their respective countries. I hadn't fully realized how close we all had become until we had to say "adieu." Through the smiles and tears we agreed to stay in touch and wished each other all success. It was a heart-wrenching moment, and again, one of those life moments that would live with me always. Laure was another matter. She was off to Avignon and was returning to the Sorbonne in the fall and we agreed to try to room together once again. My adopted sister Laure who was so happy for my happiness and I for her. She made all these plans and events even more perfect and I left the Cite with a very light heart and two very heavy trunks of clothes.

Jean Francois and I motored off to Annecy and we discovered my new home in the home of Madame Boulet, a lovely little old lady who required proper French and proper behavior of all her tenants. There were very few tenants during the summer months, however, which was fine for me as I could spend the necessary hours with my piano. The piano was just outside the door of my room and I had total access to it. This was a perfect situation for me, everything was just perfect and I told Madame so, as we shared tea and croissants. She smiled at me with her eyes just like Monsieur Gentil and Jean Francois. Is that a French characteristic I wondered?

Once settled, Madame waved her handkerchief at me and Jean Francois as we drove off for the south of France for a well deserved petite vacation of just a few days or so, as I had to return to my studies and he, his work. I had to pinch myself to come to the realization that this was all true, not just a figment of my imagination or some exotic dream. I was here, he was driving, the road coming at us was as if the future was as picturesque as the French countryside. There can be no happiness again as I felt at that moment.

The Cote d' Azure was as beautiful as I had imagined. The hills cascaded to the sea and the white beaches were full of beautiful people, scantily clad and as brown, or more brown than I. Jean Francois drove me as far south as we could go without leaving the country but, I the crazy American, had to put a toe into Italy, much to the amusement of the border guards. We took long walks at night and the lights along the shore shimmered across the waves. We walked out on the breakwater and listened to the soft splash of waves caressing the rocks and we caressed each other until there was no other place to go but home to bed.

Too soon we had to leave. Our careers called us and we returned to Annecy to my piano and Jean Francois to his company. We saw each other as often as his time permitted and the summer was fast slipping by. I was receiving marvelous technical training from Monsieur and my skills were improving at a faster rate since I was one on one with Monsieur at least once or twice a week. Having been given the opportunity to stay another year, I had to be good, I had to get it right. The pressure was on and I was not about to lose what I had. Work? God did I work!

The Cite was just as I had left it and I managed to get my old room back along with my old roommate, Laure. After a long kiss goodbye to Jean Francois, I ran the stairs to my room and there was Laure. We hugged and hugged and talked non-stop telling each other about the wonderful summer we had had. She was inviting me to go to Avignon to meet her family over Christmas break and I was thrilled. We immediately resumed our routine of speaking only French on certain days and English on others. My French was improving rapidly as I had picked up enough slang and swear words to get along with the best. It was amazing how quickly we picked up right where we had left off months before. It was good to be back.

I began to mellow as far as being in contact with my mother. As the new semester wore on I found myself writing more frequently than ever. She was well aware of my spending another year and I was hearing from her regularly as well. She kept me informed about the gossipy news and tidbits about the family but never a word about Edward, nor did I ever hear from Edward at all. That was best because neither mother nor I knew what was to become of that marriage when I returned. We just didn't face it.

Oddly enough, one day I opened my mail and found a letter from Laurie Phillips, our English shipmate friend. We had corresponded once or twice since our voyage but this letter came at a bit of a surprise because he was inviting me to London. He had told me that he wanted to show me around his beloved city when we said goodbye in Southampton and now I had the invitation in hand. I was full of hesitation because of my relationship with Jean Francois and I didn't know how he would accept the fact that I was going to see another man, platonic association or not. It was a real dilemma because if the truth were known, I really wanted to see London. I wanted to test the water but I didn't want to get burned.

I approached Jean Francois and showed him the letter and asked what he thought. I told him of my reticence and once again, as he had done so many times, he surprised me with his answer. He told me by all means to go. How would I ever see London if I didn't accept this kind offer? How would I ever find a better tour guide than Laurie? He took my head in his hands, looked deeply into my eyes and said that there was nothing in this world that would change how he felt about me. Ours was not just a love affair, not just two ships in the night. We knew each other at every level of our existence and there was no violating that intimacy. There was nothing I would ever do to hurt him and I trusted him completely. I told him how I loved him and he urged his "little cabbage" to write Laurie and make travel arrangements at once. I did so that night.

Plans had to be made around my school schedule so that I could arrange a three-day weekend and the time in early October was set. I could not spend the stipend money on the trip so, once again, Jean Francois stepped up and bought my boat-train ticket. I arrived at Charring Cross Station and there was our dear friend in all his six foot four grandeur, blonde hair flying, red face beaming. As I left the platform he swooped me off my feet and nervously told me how happy he was to see me. I forgot myself completely and began speaking in French until I realized I could now speak English. I wasn't the little American bumpkin he had met on the boat a year and a half before. I had cut my hair, I was dressed far more elegantly and had become more "Frenchized" than I had realized.

Typically Laurie, he wanted to ask me all the questions at once and it took me forever to calm him down. I don't think I had ever seen anyone so happy to see me. I didn't know quite what to think of it. We left the station and hailed a cab, which took us to his flat so that I could store my luggage. His apartment was very modest at best and a second story walk up. He wanted to know how I was doing at L'Ecole, how was it I was able to get a second year. He inquired about Jean Francois as well and I told him how Jean Francois had shown me Paris and had been such a help and wonderful friend. I didn't think it necessary or proper to tell him the extent of our intimate relationship, however I had some chances to infer that we were very close. Laurie told me of his own accomplishments; how he was to finish his fieldwork at Cambridge whereupon he would receive his PhD in Geology. There was no one in his life, which was not surprising as I knew how his shyness was disabling when it came to approaching females. Laurie was not what you call a mover and a shaker.

We left his apartment and took the "Tube" to the various sections of "London Town." Here I was in the land of tea and marmalade, "pip-pip" and "stiff upper lip." We had dinner at a lovely restaurant but I soon found out I did not like the greasy British menu. They used way too much oil and vegetables were horribly over cooked. In contrast to the French cuisine I had become accustomed to, I realized how very spoiled I had become.

The broad streets of London were total bedlam. The mere fact that they drove on the left side of the road blew my mind. Just like in Paris, everyone seemed to drive with two controls; the accelerator and the horn. We walked and walked and I marveled at the huge buildings. Big Ben loomed over the Thames River and there were such large, stone and brick edifices with massive gargoyles staring down accusingly at me. The bridges were masterpieces of architecture and the Roman Arch and I wondered if I was on the same sidewalk as Shakespeare, Chaucer, Keats and Shelly had strolled. London is history and I was loving it. All the pictures I had seen, all the books I had read, all the things I had heard about were coming alive before me.

We toured Hyde Park and I was amused at the various strange people standing on their soapboxes hawking their personal philosophies of one kind or another. Some would be railing against the government while others tried to gather an audience interested in animal rights, gay rights, civil rights or any rightful issue of the day. Free speech at its best I thought.

The time went quickly and Laurie tried his very best to make me feel interested and comfortable in "his" London, and he did. He was a perfect gentleman for the three days I was there and he tried his very best to impress me with his rather bumbling charm. Although I stayed with Laurie, we had separate sleeping arrangements; I in the bed and he on the divan. He never made any advances, for which I was eternally grateful because it was very apparent that he was in love with me and it made me somewhat uncomfortable knowing that I had no similar feelings, and yet I was accepting his hospitality. It was good for me in a way, though, in that it had become very evident that of the two men I had met on the Queen Elisabeth, Jean Francois and I were meant to be together. As much as I liked Laurie, it was perfectly clear now that I was in love with Jean Francois and there wasn't even a choice to be made. Knowing that, the parting at the train station was difficult. He had told me that he might be in Massachusetts that year on his way to Canada as part of his education. I told him that if he did so he could stay with my mother for which he was very grateful and had a difficult time finding the words to say goodbye. I was glad he couldn't, as I didn't want him to make any statements that would embarrass him or me. I thanked him profusely as he really had shown me a wonderful time. A kiss goodbye and then we agreed to stay in touch by letter. My trip home was a happy one knowing that I was returning to France and particularly "mon cher Monsieur Chivot."

Upon return to the Cite, I found everything as I had left it and I exploded upon Laure the events of the weekend and my resolve about Jean Francois. After many moments of my non-stop verbal barrage she smiled that crooked little smile of hers and said, "Of course my little Jacqui. Of course it is Jean Francois, I could have told you that. But you had to find out for yourself didn't you!"

I could not wait to see Jean Francois and I told him so on the phone that day. We made arrangements to be together when he came to Paris the following week. I couldn't wait to see him and tell him everything and assure him that he was the one I loved. I poured myself into the piano with a vengeance until that day arrived. In bed that night, I told him about all that had happened and of my assessment of London and Laurie Phillips. London, he knew all about but when it came to Laurie, be was quietly assuring me that it was all right. He didn't say anything. He just looked at me with that wonderful look that always disarmed and comforted me. His eyes always could say more than words and I was warm and safe and I knew that he loved me as much as I, him. There was not a ripple on the water. All was well.

My piano had never had the attention that I gave it in the months ahead. I was convinced that I had to overcome the shortcomings I felt at the technical level. Monsieur pointed out some of the things that required work if I were ever to be a soloist. I was determined to overcome these issues and I spent more time in the practice room than in my own room. I saw no one but Laure; I explained to Jean Francois what had to be done. With his understanding, our meetings became less frequent as I couldn't let anyone or anything stand in the way of my piano expertise. I was as close to obsession as I had ever been. Time flew by as a result and the next thing I knew Christmas was a few days away and Laure was exuberantly planning my visit to meet her family.

Victor Valay, Laure's brother drove up in his ancient automobile and I was introduced warmly to him. Laure and I had been sitting on our luggage for an hour and Victor apologized for the delay, which turned out to be due to an accident on the way. But we loaded our luggage and Victor, an affable gentleman, hopped into the driver's seat with a big smile and told us to hold on to our seats. Hold on! You bet your ass I held on! Victor drove like all the others in France, fast and with questionable control. As a result the trip to Avignon was made in record time and I found out that closing one's eyes helps with the fear factor.

Laure's family was very hospitable and made me feel at once comfortable and welcomed. They showed me to Laure's bedroom, which we were to share and then we began to know one another. They wanted to know all about this crazy, black American that Laure had been telling them about for so long. How did I like France? What were my goals with my piano? Where did I live in America? What was my family like? I, of course put on my best French and did the best I could to answer their curiosity. I felt relaxed and at ease and when I got stuck with a French equivalent, I would just look to Laure and she would bail me out with a translation. I knew at once that the week to come was going to be some pleasant down time I desperately needed.

The Valays showed me the quaint town of Avignon with its ancient churches, bakery and cheese shop and of course the famous bridge from the song, "Sur Le Pont d'Avignon." The surrounding countryside was of Impressionist grandeur with fields of vegetables and hay dotted with idle farm equipment. We took many long walks arm in arm and Laure and I became even closer than ever before. She was the older sister I never had and I was able to unload on her all the fears and misgivings that were looming on the horizon. I knew that the New Year was here and I had no chance for further extensions of my fellowship. Was I going to be able to pass my final exam? Was I going to be able to go home and start performing seriously? Did I have it as a soloist? I had designed my whole curriculum as a performance major. I wanted to perform, not just teach. It has always been said that if you can't perform, you teach, and I didn't want that said about me. What about Jean Francois and me? What was it going to be like going home to a husband I didn't really have? There seemed to be a certain finality overtaking me and I was afraid. It was Laure who brought my soul back to reality. She didn't console, she bolstered me by reminding me of how far I had come, that whatever was going to happen was going to happen and that I was doing all I could to make the outcome a positive one.

Laure took me by the shoulders and looked into my soul as she addressed the future I had with Jean Francois. She told me about the class rules in France, about what was expected of a man in his position; the son of the business owner who was to be the successor to run that business. But the rules said that a business owner was not to marry out of his class and station in life. That no matter how much he loved me, there was virtually no chance of a permanent relationship. This was as good as it was going to be. I realized then, in the crush of the moment, in the despair of possibly losing Jean Francois, what a young, naïve little girl from Dorchester I had been. My Pygmalion ambitions were being ruined by the realities of life. Oh God, had I come all this way just to lose it all? We held on to each other as I cried. Oh, how I cried.

Laure helped wipe my tears and said she had a grand surprise for me back at the house at dinnertime. She was going to brighten me up by explaining that I was going to be introduced to a delicacy of the house. The tradition in the Valay family was to start a special meal with fresh raw oysters as a first course. I was appalled! I had never had a raw oyster in my life and I wasn't about to start then. Laure explained that her parents would be insulted if I didn't join them in this family ritual. She told me how to do it. She said to take the oyster in the shell and simply throw my head back and let it slide down. "Bullshit", I said resorting to English. If I did that it would come right back up. But Laure was relentless. She said that I would have some bread and champagne so that when I took the oyster, I would immediately take a big bite of bread and then wash it all down with the champagne. Reluctantly, I mean reluctantly, I agreed.

The meal was to begin. Madame Valay was in her apron and she and Laure set the table while the men talked and I commiserated in the prospect of those goddamn oysters. The meal smelled delectable and the conversation was lively and happy but I couldn't get the goddamn oysters out of my brain. This was going to be a challenge. And they knew it. I could tell from the looks and the snickering, they knew it. The chatter continued as everyone sat at the table, the napkins tossed to the laps as eager hands reached for the first oyster. The shells had been shucked and ready for consumption and I saw the wrists in the air as everyone threw their heads back and let them slide right down just as Laure had described. Everyone, that is, but me. All eyes were on me as I reached and looked at the slimy thing in the middle of the shell and just about lost it right then and there but I had promised Laure and I didn't want to embarrass her in front of her family. I closed my eyes and lowered it to my lip and tipped it 'til it slid into my mouth. I swallowed, grabbed the bread, chased with champagne and only then did I open my eyes. Everyone laughed and clapped their hands and I did all I could to manage a smile....and to keep it down. From that moment on, I was one of them.

My resolve returned over the days to come with the dawning of the new year and I was determined to salvage all that I could despite the ill wind that was starting to blow. I returned to the Cite determined to overcome my doubts and fears and the only way I knew to do that was to play and play and play. I was ready to face anything that came my way. I was going to succeed and play as well as I possibly could but I had to face the fact that I was to lose Jean Francois.

I resumed my life at the Cite and dedicated myself to my piano with gusto I had never known before. The pressure was on; Monsieur Gentil had gone out on such a limb for me and my ambition to be a concert artist was an all-consuming passion. The weeks flew by into months and as I looked around at my peers, it was becoming clear to me that the past, the poor beginnings of my piano life were coming to haunt me. From a technical standpoint, I simply could not seem to perform those nuances that make a person either good or great. It wasn't that I couldn't play the music, it was that, in my own mind, I couldn't provide the bravado, the hudspa, the moxie that was needed to be a great soloist. I knew that even if I passed the final exams that I did not have the technical proficiency to achieve my goal. Moreover, the end was coming fast. I was to complete my exams and then return home and there was no way to have another extension. Jean Francois and I were still seeing each other and the romance was still full of passion but we both knew that the end was coming and I felt this wave of emptiness coming with each day.

The time came and I had started packing. I was packing even before the final exam because whatever the outcome, I was coming home. Laure and I stayed up and talked and talked while she smoked and I cried and cried about my fears. She was wonderful and uplifting and told me that regardless of the outcome, I had a grand talent that could be used in so many ways, not just as a soloist.

I arrived for my final exam and played to the best I could bring up considering the grim prospect facing me. I think I played well but I knew that the things that had been lacking came into the performance and although Monsieur Gentil was kind and encouraging in his remarks about my skills, he gave me enough recommendations for improvement that I knew he had seen the thin side of my exam. But it was done, I had passed the final exam and had completed all the requirements of my fellowship. I had finished all that I could possibly accomplish here in France. What I had set out to do was done. Now I had to set out to finish the relationship of a lifetime with the man I loved. How could I ever overcome losing him?

Chapter 8

I was packing for the trip home on the USS United States. Laure and I had said our goodbyes weeks ago at the Cite when we cried in each other's arms. My parting from Jean Francois is a blur. I think I have wiped it out of my consciousness because it was so desperately difficult. He had told me many of the same things that Laure had; that I should go home to the prior life I had created and go on with my music; that I had all the talent necessary to be great. Yet, the gnawing thoughts of doubt were devouring me and this had to be my worst moment ever. I took my bags down stairs, into the taxi, and as tears streamed down my cheeks, I watched my beloved Paris flash by and I was on my way.

What is this place? The boat docked at the New York pier and I disembarked and found a taxi to take me to the train station. I looked around and felt like I was in a different world; an alien. It was huge, enormous and dirty. The contrast with Paris just added to my depression. I was still thinking in French and as I looked at the people; the frumpy, poorly dressed people, I realized just how French I had become. I felt like I was on a slide and there was no way to stop.

The train ride to Boston thankfully ended, as I was exhausted, dejected and lonely. There was only one place I could go and that was straight to my mother's house. I had written that I was coming home so she knew to expect me. However, she didn't expect to see the girl that walked through the door. I was very thin, I had changed my hair color and hadn't worn a bra in France for the whole time I was there. Despite all the changes, she seemed genuinely pleased to see me. That was a surprise and a welcomed one. I had enough to deal with at that time and a critical mother would have been too much.

It was like a stranger talking to her. I would get excited about telling her something but I would lapse into French because I simply wasn't used to talking rapidly in English. I wasn't saying things right; she didn't want to listen anyway, and that was the beginning of a total breakdown in communication. I was mentally out of there. It was as though I had never left. None of the things I had done or accomplished in Paris had any impact on her. My piano talent meant absolutely nothing in her limited mind. It made me wonder why in the world she ever sent me support while I was there. She had just eliminated the past two years from memory and picked up right where we left off; totally pissed off that I had married Edward.

I called Edward and after a brief but animated conversation, he drove immediately to pick me up. Edward was Edward. He was in his flirtatious mode and acted like he was going to hit on a chick for the first time. I learned very quickly how to play the game. He was asking a lot of questions but I knew not to answer with lengthy responses. I would answer but without embellishing, and with few words. That made me very mysterious indeed.

From the concert hall to the kitchen! What the hell was I doing there? I was able to slip back into the old pattern of living but I was tripping back and forth from the present to the past two years. I had to do what I had to do but it wasn't easy and I knew that the only thing that was going to keep my sanity was my piano. In the meantime I had to deal with a husband who was a sexual gymnast and the first several days were a circus. I had had a taste of what a real loving relationship was like and this, in contrast, started the wheels turning with the knowledge that this marriage would probably not make it. Sexual gymnastics was not enough and the only immediate thing I could do was play the piano. I went to the Conservatory the next day.

The Boston Conservatory of Music smiled on me as I walked through the door for the first time since graduation. There had been changes but not many and there were many familiar faces, which gave me the first confidence boost I had had in months. I went to the front office and was fortunate to find Mr. Alphin, the President and Director of the school in his office. I spoke with him and told him what I had been doing and he was visibly impressed; to the point that he offered me a job immediately as an instructor in the Preparatory Division. There, I would be instructing school children who were not full-time students as I had been in high school, teaching them on a private basis. This was the first time I could put my feet back under the piano. Once I got the job I knew I could handle both roles, marriage and work. It was a balancing act that I could control; the teeter-totter was level.

My confidence was once again total because I knew I could teach, and I liked to teach, and even though I may not have achieved my soloist goal I could help others. That which was not given unto me would be given unto to others!

The routine was good for me and it gave me the stability I needed. Edward was working a little here and a little there but, typically, never a regular job. His mother, Amelia, also typically, had bought a four-unit apartment and had given it to her precious son. We moved into one of the upstairs units where he was to manage the complex. Manage hell! Edward wasn't allowed to do anything without mama's approval. She called all the shots. If there were ever two people who hated each other with gusto, it was Amelia and me. So I stayed out of it simply to avoid contact with her. In the meantime, Edward senior had left the military and was on his way to a law career, which took him to be the

Assistant District Attorney of the Commonwealth of Massachusetts and eventually a Judge of the Superior Court. Edward's sisters had become the debutantes of the middle class black community. Mercifully I only had to put up with these nasty people when they held their gruesome family reunions. The exception was Edward senior who I had always liked and respected.

Teaching was becoming a real pleasure for me. It was becoming apparent that my style and methods were having a positive effect on these young students. It was also very apparent that I was gaining a great deal of satisfaction in their progress. I was "giving unto others" and loving it. Life was looking up.

My courage was returning and I took a big step by putting a notice on the Conservatory bulletin board offering my services as an accompanist. To my delight I received a response from one of the students who needed an accompanist for his undergraduate recitals. This was the first time I had worked as an independent professional and I took it very seriously. Here again I was enjoying what I was doing and, "giving unto others." I didn't know it then but this was the theme that was to control the rest of my professional life.

One student led to another and I started to attend their private lessons. They knew my work ethic and that I was willing to attend at any location. Also, my fees were very reasonable considering I was being paid for a second education. Their instructors were members of the Conservatory faculty but also, and more importantly, members of the Boston Symphony Orchestra. I was accompanying these students in a teaching scenario taught by the best that Boston had to offer. I soon found that I was learning as much as the students; not from books but from actual practice. I also got the information

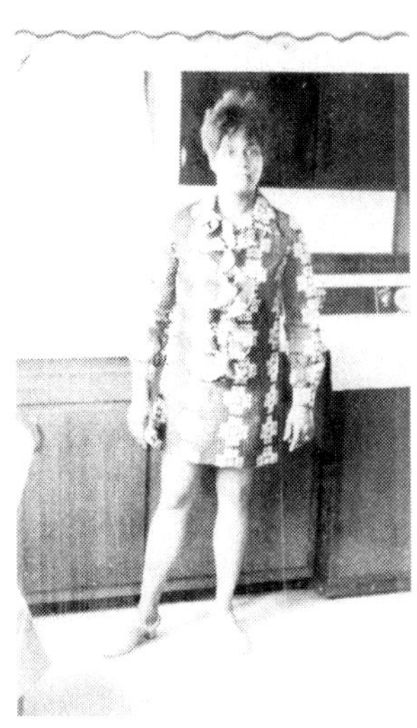

Being domestic with child

necessary to learn all about the various instruments. To accompany a cello is not the same as to accompany a bassoon or an oboe.

Everything was getting into order. I had everything and everyone in their little nook and cranny; my mother here; Edward's mother here; Edward here; my piano there. The waters of life were smooth and flowing and it was almost becoming a complacency when, wham! The fickle finger of fate was to point at me and screw everything up…..I was pregnant!

Chapter 9

Oh my god, I'm pregnant! Edward seemed pleased but I just couldn't believe the waters of my smooth existence had been rippled. But like everything else in my life, I just buried the difficulty and got on with it. Mother was overwhelmed with joy. She had had so many pregnancies that failed, she was delighted that she was going to be a grandmother. I was the only pregnancy that had made it and consequently the only one who could give her a grand child. Amelia's daughter had already made her a grandmother so as far as Edward and I were concerned, our child was anticlimactic. It was just not a big deal.

My work progressed normally and I was getting bigger and bigger, normally. When you are an accompanist you can't just say, "Sorry, I can't help you anymore. I'm going to have a baby." It is a huge responsibility because an accompanist must allow the soloist to star in the performance. I had to compliment that performance and the soloist had to rely on and trust me to enhance, not detract. It is a symbiotic relationship and a poor accompanist can ruin the performance of an excellent soloist. It is a matter of absolute trust and familiarity, which can only be accomplished by continuous rehearsal and hard work. I knew I was in my element and my piano was once again the pill I took for discontent; my anti-inflammatory.

Velicia, my first and only surviving child was supposed to come in September but she arrived on August twenty fourth 1960, sometime in the evening. I was home when my water broke and we called the hospital, which, in turn, called our Dr. Kaplan. We drove very quickly to the hospital as Edward had a racecar mentality and I was immediately admitted. Dr. Kaplan arrived and they wheeled me down the corridor and I swore to myself that I was not going to scream like what I was hearing coming out of some of the birthing rooms. They gave me an epidural which eased the pain and after a reasonable time Velicia Ayn Gourdin made a head first, normal and grand entrance into this world. Six pounds and an ounce or two with a crop of nice black hair. Not a long child considering the Gourdin genetics but a beautiful little girl. She had delicate features and after I counted all the toes and fingers, I realized I had just given birth to a healthy and lovely baby. I was in awe that she came out of me, that she was made of me, and that we could do something like this. Giving life is a spiritual thing and I was very thankful for it. Only a baby could bring Willie Fontaine, my mother and Amelia Gourdin into the same room without killing each other or at least starting an argument. But there they were, both women and the men; two Edwards and a James. Everyone smiling and "oooing and aaahing" over the baby. I was feeling just fine and after only two or three days, I was discharged and sent home. The big decisions were being made so that Velicia could be accommodated into our lifestyle. First of all, I was not going to breast feed since my intention was to get back to work as soon as possible. Secondly, my mother was perfectly willing to take care of the baby while I was at work.

Edward wasn't very happy about my going back to work but he wasn't willing to do much about getting a paying job of any kind so he couldn't protest too loudly. If I wasn't back to work, we couldn't make it financially so it wasn't an issue. I was once again learning about Edward and the way he operated. There was no way in hell that he could ever achieve even a small part of what his father had achieved and he knew it. Therefore he would imagine grandiose things about what he was going to do without a thought as to what it would take to do them. For instance, one time he went around the corner and declared he was in the real estate business but when he was asked about his real estate license, he responded, "What license?" No, I was the mainstay of the family income and all Edward could do was go to mommy when he really wanted something…..much to the disappointment of his father, the judge.

The neighborhood we lived in was predominantly Jewish, and wonderfully Jewish. I had formed a chamber trio with associates at school consisting of violin, cello and of course, my piano. The piano was in the front room of our apartment and in the summer, we would get together to rehearse with all the windows wide open. The entire neighborhood would show up and sit on the front steps to listen. We would finish a piece to firm and polite applause. They were all speaking Yiddish so I couldn't understand what they were saying but words weren't necessary. We were truly appreciated and people would wave and smile at me out in the yard or on the street. This was very important for me because no one in my house or in my family appreciated or understood my ability. As a matter of fact I was looked down upon. Edward was always off somewhere else supposedly playing jazz. One time he would come home with a guitar; next a saxophone; next time a drum. He played at all those things but never well. I'm convinced his musical attempts were simply to compete with me. All of which drove me deeper and deeper into my music; my piano.

I'm working, I'm performing, I'm teaching and I have Velicia, and as a result I was relatively happy. However, Edward and I were arguing more and more frequently. I was forced to go to his parents' house from time to time and it wasn't a happy household. It was apparent they didn't like me at all and they showed it. I was, frankly, treated like a piece of shit and I couldn't stand going over there. I was becoming very concerned about my marriage but I didn't know how to deal with it. So, like many other problems in my life, I pushed it under the chair because I didn't know what to do. My music had now become virtually everything to me because I was incapable of handling day-to-day situations.

Velicia was a happy, beautiful baby and she enjoyed being with my mother because Willie had taken in other children, some were her foster children. Mother knew how to take care of babies and, thank God, because I didn't. She was growing strong, tall and healthy and as happy a baby as I had ever seen. She was not a crying child and she smiled much of the time. Things were working out as far as Velicia was concerned.

I had been caught up in all the busyness of being a mother and trying to handle a marriage that was deteriorating almost on a daily basis. My mind would return to Jean Francois on an equally daily basis. I had been corresponding with him on several occasions but this time I wrote with the fervent intent of reuniting and rekindling that love that I had known and longed for again. Not long afterward I received his reply letter. It was not what I had hoped for because although he restated his love for me, he was well aware of Velicia and he would never be able to interfere with my marriage or my daughter. That was the kind of man he was. He had more character than anyone I had known. He wrote that some day his business would take him back to America and that maybe we could see one another but that we would never have what we once had. He was there and I was here and the things that kept us apart would never change. He wanted me to keep the memories alive and that although he had seen other women, there would never be another "My little Jacqui." I was devastated! I cried, how I cried but I couldn't let anyone know why. I had missed him so ever since I had left Paris and the emptiness was always there and now I knew I would have that emptiness forever. Once again, I turned to my only true friend, my piano and when I played they didn't know why I was playing but I was playing with all the love that was in me, my love for Jean Francois.

One fine day, Edward's mother announced to us that the building we were living in was to be sold. I suspect Edward hadn't handled things very well because she said it was a bad investment. Edward senior had bought some substantial property, including their summer home, on Cape Cod in Marstons Mills and our lives were to take another abrupt turn.

My Edward had finally taken a job, much to my amazement, at the Boston Edison Company. He was working in the vehicle maintenance department and I had thought he had finally found something that could use his skills with cars. Edward and his mother had decided, however, that we were going to move to Marstons Mills permanently. They would build us a house on the property, Edward could watch his parents' house in the winters when they were back in Boston. They also decided that Velicia would have a much better opportunity for education in the Cape Cod schools.

I went up in smoke. I couldn't imagine a move like that and what it was going to do to my music. We fought and argued continually but I couldn't compete with the Gourdin triumvirate, of which I was not a part. I mentally started to figure out how I could continue my musical career and care for Velicia at the same time. The die was cast, however, as Amelia got her boy a mortgage to build our house by co-signing the papers and construction began. We would go down on weekends to monitor the progress. We would stay in the parents' "big house" until our house was completed to the point we could move in. We finally moved down to the new house before it was actually finished and that was when Edward decided he was going to complete it himself. Holy shit, he had never done anything like that in his life but like everything else he had ever tried, he just convinced himself that he could do anything, anything at all. The reality is that the house was never finished and whatever he tried to do turned into crap. Nothing fit, nothing got painted, in the end it looked like a gingerbread house. I was miserable.

I made arrangements with the Conservatory to continue teaching on a part time basis and Edward continued working for Edison but the commute was very difficult for us both. I would drop Velicia off at my mother's, go to work, pick her up at the end of the day, drive home and look for Edward to drag himself home from a long day fixing trucks. This all came to an end when Velicia was old enough to start kindergarten. I knew I had to be there for her so commuting was no longer possible. I asked the Conservatory to cut down on the number of students but I kept my toe in the water by continuing to accompany. In that manner, I was able to stay associated with the school. Edward had whined enough to his mother that she went out and bought him a business. She bought him the Gulf Oil gas station in Mashpee, the community right next door. So, Edward resigned at Edison and we were dedicated Cape Cod'ers.

It was a whole new world. For the first time in my life my piano had to take a back seat to other matters; namely Velicia. She was growing fast, doing well in school, had good friends and generally took the move in as much stride as a five year old could. Edward was starting off with the gas station very well. He had contracts with the snow plowers, police cruisers and the tow trucks. He had a helper and together they did minor car repair.

My major problem at this point was living next door to my mother-in-law. I had to face this smug, aristocratic, condescending woman almost every day. Edward had an older sister, Betty, who was a psychologist. She would come to visit and tell everyone that I was emotionally unstable and incapable of raising a child. Consequently they all treated me like I was a mental patient and whatever I said or did made no difference whatsoever. It dated back to the fact that I came from across the tracks and Amelia couldn't believe how her dear boy could ever have married such a person. I just turned my attention to Velicia who was actually my savior. When it came to identity, I was Velicia's mother and that was something they couldn't deny or take away. Edward and I were continuing to fight on a regular basis and between him and his family I was getting beaten down.

Time went on and when Velicia was in second grade, I became pregnant again and I don't know how I felt about it. But the baby came too soon. I was only six months along and there was nothing they could do in those days to save one so early. I didn't know enough to realize what something like this could do to me but suddenly I found myself in a deep, dark depression. I would get up in the morning after drinking too much the night before, get Velicia ready for school and off on the bus and then just sit, smoke cigarettes and stare out the window. I wondered why I was here. Would I ever be loved like Jean Francois had loved me? At least in Boston I was with people who treated me like a human being but here I was treated like low-class scum. It all went back to the fact that they were Cuban blacks and I was African American. I was in agony and I couldn't make contact with my husband on anything that mattered. The only contact was sex and, of course, that was the only reason we were together in the first place.

More bad news was that Edward senior was ill. As a consequence, all of Amelia's attention turned to him. If I had been ignored before, now I was invisible. The Gourdin family, including Edward had to handle the problem of serious illness and I was left with no one but my daughter and it turned out she was the only thing that kept my sanity. I would go to her dance classes and her school plays and she was my daughter, not theirs, and as a result I was able to keep it all together.

One day, one of the parents at Velicia's school asked me to play for the children's' dance classes. I said yes and started playing for them on a weekly basis. It was fun for me to watch Velicia but, more importantly, it got my ass off the couch and back to reality. It turned out to be the first positive event in a very bleak existence and the start of the resurrection of my piano.

At first I didn't know if just playing for a dance studio was going to be enough but once I started I realized that any playing, any playing at all was the catalyst I needed to get motivated again. The more I played, the more I wanted to play and I looked forward to every class with enthusiasm. The dance teacher was a lovely woman and it worked out really well in that she would take Velicia while I was playing for the other students. It was during this time that Velicia and I became very close; as close as we had ever been.

Edward had come up with some sort of a piano so I had something to practice on and slowly, ever so slowly I was coming out of my depression. One day I was speaking with someone at the dance studio and they told me about the Cape Cod Conservatory of Music. It was in Barnstable, which wasn't too far from the house. I took my resume and portfolio and made an appointment for an interview. I think it was a Mr. McCarthy or something and he was dressed very nicely in a suit and I was dressed for the interview. Having still been associated with the Boston Conservatory served me well and I got the job. Hallelujah! I was back in business.

Contrary to all the racial tensions in the country at that time, my being black served me well also. It was true then and it is true today that my being black has been an asset, not a liability. It is because I'm the only one in the room and people are drawn to that. People found out there was a new teacher on the staff and that I was black and that I wore dungarees to work. They flocked to me. I was a magnet. I wore dungarees because we had goats at home and I would have to feed them. I was a rural person, not one of the hoity-toity Bostonians dressed in suits or skirts. I was down to earth and they knew I knew the piano.

I built the number of students rapidly and it gave me the confidence back that had fled me and had left me in the throes of despair. I found me again, I was Jacqui Gourdin and in the face of the family crap I was facing; Edward senior's illness, my sick marriage, Amelia's disdain for me; all of the things that had driven me inside of myself were becoming less and less of a drain on my self-esteem. They couldn't hurt me anymore, I could overcome that crap! I had given the name Gourdin some meaning. People appreciated what I was doing and they respected me for it. That respect, that appreciation made everything the family tried to destroy come back in spades. I was not only me again, I was a better "Me" than ever before. This was a major turning point. There would be no more wallowing in self-pity as long as I continued my craft; as long as I had my piano.

Chapter 10

Things were moving along well at the Conservatory and I had built the number of students significantly in the several years I had been there. There was trouble brewing, however, in that people would call in and ask for me while other instructors were not getting as many new pupils. This obviously created some animosity and jealous comments. All of a sudden the environment changed. I found that some people had called in asking for me and they were told that my schedule was full and they would give the student to someone else. I was asked to conform to the dress code when little did they know that I had never conformed to anything before in my life. But no more dungarees and I realized the handwriting was on the wall, I had to leave. That didn't really bother me though because I knew that I could open my own studio and do very well; not just very well, but much better. I left the Cape Cod Conservatory under very good terms, it was a cordial parting of the ways and by starting to teach out of the house, I made more money, made my own schedules and could be home for Velicia when she got out of school. It was a good change but now I had to deal with Edward. He had found a girlfriend! She had been the girlfriend of the man who worked for him at the garage but she took a liking to Edward and he to her and soon the helper was gone. Everyone knew he was seeing her and his behavior was typically obvious. He was coming home late or not at all and was very vague about his comings and goings. I found that when I would leave for work, she would come right in the back door. What made it worse was that Velicia would see what was going on. I reacted at the time typically by brushing it under the chair and trying to ignore it.

Right in the midst of all this happening, Edward senior's illness turned critical and I had lost the only member of the Gourdin family that had treated me kindly. It was a sad day when he died and I couldn't even face going to the funeral. I grieved him in my own way and didn't have to face the family doing it. Now it was just Edward, his mother and his sister, Dr. Elizabeth Gourdin. Without my buffer, Edward senior, I was alone in a snake pit.

I couldn't sweep the marriage under the chair anymore. The girlfriend had moved down from Boston, set up residence and they were seeing each other on a regular basis. I knew it was over. I went to Edward and told him I was divorcing him and moving out. Now this is how the dumb shit thinks......he said that I didn't have to divorce, just move out. In that way he could move her in and screw her but if she wasn't available he could come and screw me because I was still his wife. He had another thing coming; I filed for divorce and moved out.

Oh God, did I move out! I was telling one of my clients that I needed a place to stay and she turned out to be a real estate agent. She called one day and said she had the perfect place for me right across the road in Cotuit. I took Velicia and we went to see the apartment. It was perfect. It was in a huge house owned by a Jewish family. (I don't know why Jewish families always enter my life, but they did and they do) It had two bedrooms, two bathrooms, a garage underneath and a beautiful two-sided fireplace where we could watch the fire from either the living room or the dining room. In addition there were wonderful glass windows looking out upon a beautiful, thick forest. All of which was topped off with the fact that there was a Steinway grand piano in the living room. God was with me that day...or was it you father? I was in heaven.

You don't know how much people know about your circumstances but when I moved out and filed for divorce, it was like I had a cheering section behind me. Everyone was so supportive and told me how pleased they were that I had finally done something and that did my heart a great deal of good. It also did my heart good when Edward drove his truck full of my things and saw where I was going to be living. I saw the look of envy in his face. He didn't expect me to do well but I was doing well and it would never include him again. Yes, my heart was doing well.

It really amazes me that Edward never fought the divorce. He just wanted the convenience of having two women around to which he could spread his sexual appetite. The court was very much in my corner because Edward simply would never show up for hearings but when all was said and done, I was awarded something like twenty-five dollars a week for Velicia and I soon found out he wouldn't even pay that. He certainly couldn't go to his mother and ask her for alimony for me. I was on my own.

I was dedicated to getting on with my life. Velicia and my piano were the only things I had to concentrate on and love. Cotuit was a stone throw away so I didn't lose any students and my student base was growing nicely and I knew I was doing the right thing. But I was still in a great deal of pain. I came home from Europe deeply hurt by losing Jean Francois and I had convinced myself that I was going to be with Edward and that I would never leave him. After all we were married and I wanted to pick up the pieces and make it work. Now that this had also fallen apart, I had the miserable feeling that I was all used up and that I was no good to any man. At my age, with Velicia, and all the baggage I was carrying, I was still somewhat depressed with the feelings of inadequacy. Not like before. I had brought myself out of that hole but there was a hole I was still trying to climb out of. My piano was the only ladder I had.

My connections in Falmouth had put my name about and I had become known as the best teacher they knew. Soon I was in demand in Falmouth and we needed a place for me to teach and that is when they suggested St. Barnabas Episcopal Church right in the main street of town. I met the Rector, Father Crowell and he was immediately in favor of my using the Rectory for teaching and also for performances. It was then I knew I had to have a reasonable piano I could trust and that is when I found "Baby" in Boston on Boylston Street at a music store that sold pianos and organs. I walked into the store and obviously they were not accustomed to a black person shopping for a piano. Especially not a young, single black person. The gentleman approached me and asked what I was looking for and I told him a "grand" piano and he seemed a little reluctant but showed me the various pianos in the first room of pianos. They were beautiful. He let me sit and play one or two and when he heard me play he obviously knew I was serious and a capable pianist. Suddenly his reluctant demeanor changed and he knew he had a live one. I looked from piano to piano and the price tags were scaring the hell out of me. The store was long and narrow; a series of connected rooms with varying displays of pianos; all sizes and shapes and makes. I was like a kid in a candy store and examined each one carefully. Finally we reached the last room and he opened the door and there in front of me was the piano of my dreams. She was beautiful! A Yamaha C3 and brand spanking new. How was I to know then that she would become the most valuable thing? I sat down to her, this bright, beautiful piano and when I started to play, I instantly knew she was it. The music rang in the room, it was a powerful sound and aggressive as I am aggressive and we fit. God, I knew it in a moment we fit. I wanted to get to know her immediately. I walked around her examining every inch. I looked inside of her and underneath her and looked at my image on her shined ebony surface. This was my piano, my "Baby".

It was a very difficult decision, however, in that I also needed a car. After divorcing Edward I had no way of getting around except when people could drive me, which was not a good situation. My God, what was I to buy? A piano I needed for subsistence and my musical well being and therapy or a lousy car that would get me around from bad piano to bad piano.

There are a couple of miracles that happened at that time; one I decided to buy her and; two, they let me. After all my finances were not in the best of shape; I was just divorced; I was self-employed and I owned no real estate or anything of great value to back up my request for credit. I don't know what they checked or how they checked my application but I was absolutely elated when they said Baby was mine. I had her shipped home and had her placed at the church where I knew she was safe and in addition I put a lock on her so no one could play but me.

Some of the most vile moments I endured were when Edward's girlfriend, Debbie, would drive past our house in Cotuit and actually wave to me out the window of her brand new God damned Chrysler automobile that was bigger than a bus. More than once she would arrive at an affair where Velicia was involved and she would be clinging to his arm to show that she was now Edward's woman. Edward knew I needed a car and every time he visited Velicia I would mention it to him. Finally, one time he said he was going to give me the old Ford that I used to drive when we were married. It was old and purple but Edward, being a mechanic, kept it in good shape and it solved a big problem. He gave me the car to look good in Velicia's eyes and also to cover for the fact he wasn't paying any child support, but I thanked him anyway. Now I could think about moving off the Cape, I had mobility.

I couldn't believe how fast the years had flown as I drove out of Cotuit for the last time. The old purple car was filled with everything I owned plus Velicia and three cats. But everything I owned wasn't very much since all that Edward and I ever had was bought by his mother so he kept it all. The weather was really hot, around ninety degrees and as we drove up the South Shore, we realized that the cats had peed all over the back seat of the car. These were Siamese cats and their urine is very strong and they were nervous about the move, so pee they did. It was a long drive to say the least but we somehow made it.

I had put Baby in storage, called my mother and suggested that we buy a house and as miracles continued to happen, she agreed. Another miracle was that she was willing to cash in an insurance policy for the down payment and I had the credit with which to apply for a mortgage. The biggest miracle was that the South Boston Savings Bank, which is located in the midst of the Irish Catholic neighborhood, actually approved the loan. There was a time when they wouldn't have even allowed me to apply. This was right in the middle of the black power movement and maybe they did it for political reasons but the point is that I got the mortgage. We had both been looking for a house to buy. Mother had some contacts in the black community and one of them was a real estate agent who found a very nice home in the Field's Corner section of Dorchester.

Living with mother and James was a study in chaos and although we never killed one another, the old arguments continued on a regular basis and murder was a viable alternative. Mother never let James near the negotiations for the house considering his absolute inability to do anything constructive requiring money.

He had lost one house for her and she wasn't about to let it happen again. It was a real blessing when the closing came together and papers were signed and we were able to move into our new home. The house was very spacious with a total of six bedrooms, two bathrooms and enough room for Willie and James to occupy the two top floors while Velicia and I occupied the main floor, which also had large rooms for my music studio.

The transition to our new home took some time but went relatively smooth. I had enrolled Velicia in a private school called the Windsor School whose graduates could gain any Ivy League school they desired. Expensive, God yes, but much better than the alternative of the Boston Public Schools which were enforcing bussing and not without some violence and a lot of strain. I was back at the Boston Conservatory and it was as if I had never left. They had known me since the fifties and I was a fixture on the wall. Now it was time for Baby. I sent for her and waited nervously for her arrival and finally the day came. The professional piano movers exercised extra care delivering her considering I threatened emasculation if anything bad happened. Nothing did and I tipped them both handsomely. Baby and I were back together again and we were to start on another journey in this life, together. I cleaned her, kissed her and played for hours. Everything was complete, I had overcome and survived it all. I was happy once again.

Chapter 11

I had forgotten what it was like living with my mother. Even though she was living two floors above me, she seeped through the floorboards and inundated my entire space. She would rant and rave about every little thing that went wrong and she had this driving compulsion to control everything in the house, including me. She would tell me how to do things, when to do things and why I was to do them. With the ten-inch index finger wagging in front of my face, she would remind me of all the mistakes I had ever made in my life. I should never have married Edward; I should never have married into that goddamn Cuban family who thought they were white and I should never have moved to the Cape.

Willie had to be shut out of my consciousness and I had to get things organized in my life. First, Velicia had to get into school and get on a schedule, next I made sure that I was settled at the Conservatory and then the concentration was on building the student base at home. All of these things were going well and I was on my way to providing a good living for the entire household. A fact of which I was never given credit.

Willie had foster children from day one. It is an odd thing but she would be sure that the foster children were all males. She had to be sure that she was regarded as the queen of the house and she wanted no competition from females. There was also that old southern attitude that girls were dirty and had periods, which were dirty, and all they wanted to do was have babies. Really a bunch of crazy crap, but that was her. There were always two or three little boys in the house and they were under strict instructions not to disturb my teaching. They would play in the front yard or the back yard and only came into my part of the house when I wanted to give them something or talk to them about something. Velicia was kind of a big sister figure and she seemed to get along very well with them.

Weekends were the usual firefights, skirmishes and out and out knock down-drag outs; usually over money. Fontaine was working here and there and brought home some fairly significant money. Willie, of course, would battle to get the most she could from him to run the house and you could hear them yell at each other all over the neighborhood. Fontaine was always good to me. His nickname for me was "Poodle" and he always gave me a smile and a kind word. The man drank a great deal of whiskey however. Not good whiskey, it was what we would call "rot gut." He would sit there and drink and smoke his cigarettes until he was numb. I think Fontaine drank like that so he could shut out my mother. He could never get anything out of his mouth without Willie correcting him or belittling him. That was his life and as a consequence he started to go out and drink and then we had the worry about whether he was going to get home in one piece or not. She was as awful to him as she was to me.

I was able to shut most of this out now that I was so involved at the Conservatory and with my students at home. My life was full and my time very occupied. The months were flying by and we each had our schedules and agendas that we followed in the ebb and flow of daily life. I wasn't in a rut but maybe a groove of routine when many of my friends at the Conservatory recommended that I go back to school and get my masters degree. With a masters I could get a job at a university, hopefully on the faculty but at least on the adjunct faculty.

It was at this time I met Peter Lancto, a tuba player whom I was accompanying. Peter was a mountain of a man, really big, with bright blue and sparkling eyes. He was so good to me and we became instant friends. He wouldn't let me wallow in the home scene and complain; he would make light of those things and bring me back to reality. He was an excellent tuba player and performed with local symphonies, operas and brass bands. He was also a music educator who had a wonderful manner with children and adults alike. I loved accompanying him and we became very close. Peter, among others, was instrumental in my decision to return to school at the University of Lowell and upon his advice I applied for a position on the faculty. It was then they realized that I did not have my Masters Degree so they said that if I got the job I would have to enroll for the Masters program but it would be tuition free. I was elated considering the cost of the two-year program. The miracles continued.

I was at the right place at the right time at Lowell. The school was part of the entire Massachusetts education system and had definite requirements for hiring minorities and enrolling student minorities as a part of their Affirmative Action Program. I was perfect because I satisfied several requirements. I was a student but I could also teach plus I was female and black. As a part of the entrance requirements, I was required to play in front of a panel of nine members of the Performance Department faculty. Oddly enough I was just as nervous before playing before this group as I was at L'Ecole Normale in Paris. The outcome was just as good, however, as everyone on the panel but one approved my appointment to the Adjunct Faculty. I was off and running.

Dr. Espinoza stared at me as I entered the classroom the first day and not very pleasantly. It was quite apparent that I was the oldest person in the class; even older than Ms. Espinoza, PhD. As the semester began I became aware of the fact that the modern methods of teaching were not mine. In those days I was quite lenient and had a tendency to give the benefit of the doubt.

Peter, Brian and I performing

Not Senorita Espinoza; she was tough and I soon realized that I may have a problem with her. One day we met on the elevator and she told me that in the Masters program, we had to achieve grades of B+ or better or we would have to repeat the course. Then she surprised me by saying that I may want to discontinue her course. She said she didn't like the answers I gave in regard to instructing at the college level; that I was all right for elementary or high school but not college. Just before the door opened, I was able to tell her that she didn't know me; that I didn't quit and if I didn't achieve a B+ she would see my smiling face in her class next semester. My back was burning as I left the elevator.

I somehow passed her course with a great deal of help from Peter. The course was Research and Bibliography, which brought students back to the origins of classical music, which is predominantly German. Peter knew German and would help me with my papers and presentations. God love him, he was an angel sent to me. My angel Peter was also helping me to grow up in the music world. Just as I had to grow up from Edward, I had to grow up in my music.

For most people, graduation from an advanced degree program is a day of celebration but for me it was a day of victory, victory over an educational system that was politically run by the very same man, Dr. Lindblad who had voted against me following my audition. I don't know if it was my race or age or both but I had just spent two years of my life bucking the Espinozas and the Lindblads in the world of academia and I won. I beat them at their own game and I didn't have to change Jacqui Gourdin one iota. There was no way I was going to a goddamn graduation ceremony sitting in the hot sun and waiting for my name to be called and having a damned tassel bouncing in my face. I was victorious and a girlfriend and I went out to lunch and later I wore my best dress to the administration office and they simply handed me my diploma without any ceremony and that was that.

The next months and years of my career at Lowell were a definite step up for me. I did a great deal of performing while developing another one piano/four hand team with Juanita Tsu, a member of our piano faculty. We played frequently at school as well as public

One Piano/Four Hands with Juanita Tsu

performances in Boston. She was a real firebrand with a high energy level like mine and she played with excellent technique. Peter was always there and we performed on many occasions and my relationship with him grew closer and closer. Peter was not only my partner but my mentor and his encouragement meant a great deal to me. The classes under my instruction were full and the students seemed to like my style of instruction, which, contrary to Ms.Espinoza, was very effective at the college level.

Our lives finally had gained a somewhat comfortable and stable level. Velicia was doing well in high school, my relationship with Willie had its normal ups and downs but we had had no major conflicts. Life was good and peaceful again.

One of the saddest things at that time was what was becoming of Jesse, my cousin/brother/childhood sibling. He had gone into the army and went off to the Korean conflict and when he came back it was apparent that he had changed dramatically. That warm and loving child had turned into an angry and somewhat frightful man. He had married and he did not get along well at all with his in-laws and when his wife gave him a baby, her parents stepped into the marriage and smothered the little boy, David, by spoiling him rotten. The boy was being raised primarily by women and Jesse was purposely left out of the picture which is a continuance of the way he was raised by his mother, Birdell and my mother Willie. All of this added up to a dysfunctional marriage and Jesse's anger increased to the point that his wife and even I were afraid of him. He would fly into tirades at the slightest provocation and that was when he became violent. He beat his wife once too often and she divorced him soon after. Our relationship soon widened as well as it was hard to be close to him in that state of mind and the physical distance increased also as he started moving from pillar to post.

There was one occasion, however, where Jesse tried to help me. I asked him to speak to my mother about modifying the house to include an apartment or two to help with the finances. He sat there talking with her pointing out that I was the only one providing for the household and that he thought that she was paying much more attention to the foster children than she did me. He told her that I went to work every day, brought the money home to pay the bills, never brought bad people into the home and frankly was working my ass off to support her and hers. It didn't even faze her, she would have none of it and it all stemmed back to the fact that her name wasn't on the deed to the house. He gave up trying and so did I and I pulled in, as is my way, and gave up on the whole idea. The last I heard Jesse married again at least once, had more children who got into drugs and all sorts of trouble and it finally came to the point where I had to give up on my brother. It is very sad to say.

My life would have been perfect if it hadn't been for my family. Of all the discordant influences in my life, Birdell had to be it. I hated to see the holidays come because she and Hazel and Willie would get together and it was reminiscent of Sarasota when I was a little girl. They would sit around and argue about the most trivial things. How old was Grandma? He didn't say that! She was the one who did that? The arguments grew to the point where it would get physical and we almost had to call the police. No wonder Jesse was as he was.

The winter of nineteen seventy-eight was brutal and Boston suffered one of the worst snowstorms in its history. No one could go anywhere for days. We were all snowbound. One day Birdell called Willie and they were having one of their marathon conversations when

Birdell made a strange sound and went silent. Willie went to another phone and called the fire department. Birdell had been living in a high rise apartment where doors could only be opened from the inside. They put up a ladder to her window and gained entrance that way and found Birdell dead on the floor. She had suffered a massive heart attack and died instantly. Willie and Jesse handled all the arrangements. Birdell had used up a number of churches because she changed churches like you change your socks but the last one was a Seventh Day Adventist Church in the South End. They were really off the wall. They called her Sister Toomer and conducted what I call 'woo woo' services and I didn't even go to pay respects. I have a great deal of trouble going to funerals and especially for people who had caused me so much grief.

Chapter 12

My life on Larchmont Street became a relatively steady routine. I was teaching at Lowell and at home so the financial situation had become sufficient and stable also. Willie and Fontaine had their turbulent lives on the upper floors and I on the first. We would interact only as necessary and I really didn't want to spend very much time with them. I didn't have much time to spend to begin with and Willie and James had the three foster boys that occupied a great deal of their time as well.

Velicia graduates from high school

Willie was also taking in day care kids from the neighborhood so she was very busy and James just sat and drank and smoked so he really wasn't a factor.

The years flew by. Velicia graduated from high school and applied to the Pratt Institute in Brooklyn, New York and was accepted. She was to study fashion illustration and design. It was a full course with all the allied subjects like photography and layout. She enjoyed the school but after her first year I was getting calls of real distress and eventually of out and out fear. She was living with roommates who would use her things, break her things or steal them. They were bringing people home to the room she didn't know, smoking dope and they were generally a sleazy lot. One night she woke up in the middle of the night to see a man sitting on her bed, smoking weed and looking lustily at her. That and the cockroaches and rats and frightening company caused her to call me in tears. I told her that if she was concerned about her safety and well-being, she better get her ass home NOW. I told her that if she did, she could enter school in Boston and live at home. I would clothe her, feed her and generally support her but she would have to get a part time job to cover school expenses.

Home came Velicia and I set her up in a small bedroom in my part of the house. She contacted her old high school friends at Windsor and they put her in touch with the New England School of Art and Design. She applied, was accepted and received scholarship money for her talent, her grades and because I was a single, black mother. She started school and then went out and got herself a fantastic job at the Greyhound Bus Lines. She was a union employee and made fantastic money; actually more than I was making. She was as happy as she could be. Her health improved, she was no longer afraid to go out and she seemed to have many friends. She graduated with her degree in Fine Art and went to work for a fashion house that gave her the freedom of design that made her work very special. I was very proud of her when she had some of her work show up in the Boston Globe and a number of fashion magazines. Velicia was extremely creative and could have gone on to have her own fashion house with her name on everything. But it was then she met a man named "Petey" Peters, who after dating for some time, swept her off her feet. They decided to live together.

They were living in a small apartment in the Back Bay, not far from the Conservatory and Velicia still had her job but Petey lost his at the Neiman Marcus Department Store and they lost the apartment. Their only recourse was to move in with Petey's mother but in order to do so they had to get married as mama wasn't about to let her little boy sleep with some girl in her house.

The Episcopal Church of Roxbury was this rambling, stuccoed building with the typical English wood façade. Velicia had made her own gown and it and she were stunning. She knew what looked good on her body and she virtually designed and made her entire wedding gown from scratch. When she walked down that isle her eyes sparkled. I had never seen Edward look so good either. He wore a tuxedo and a huge smile as he took her arm and led her to the alter. I wore an orchid chiffon dress with matching shoes and corsage and I felt lovely too. She had four bridesmaids and Petey four groomsmen all of whom were young, pretty and handsome. The flowers were bright, fragrant and everywhere, and the church was full. Petey's family was Portuguese and the Portuguese don't particularly like blacks but because Velicia came from a Cuban background, she was accepted. I on the other hand was whale shit on the bottom of the sea; not only because I was black but because I was considered high brow since I was a concert pianist. I had been through this before with Edward's family and I was learning to play the game. So I communicated in a very controlled and unemotional fashion and simply ignored the subtle snobbery. I was not alone at the wedding; I had my piano and Peter and I played for the soloist who was a friend of mine and Velicia's. She had a beautiful voice and we sounded the best a piano and voice can sound.

The reception was at a local hall in Roxbury where Petey's father had provided an open bar of which everyone took strong advantage. The band was good and Peter was by my side. The bride and groom danced and the floor was full from then on. Peter and I giggled and danced and kicked up and had a wonderful time. He was always like that and it was one of the reasons we got along so well. Velicia thanked me for the wedding and I drank some more and Peter took me home…thank heaven.

Now Velicia was grown and gone and had a life of her own to look forward to. She and Petey moved in with his parents who were ecstatic to have son and daughter-in-law to control. Petey's mother ran everything and the father was a mute member of the house. I returned to my piano with a new sense of relief. It was strange to feel a certain amount of relief when I had virtually lost a child but I had so damn much family in my house that one moving out had given me appreciation of the added space; physical space and emotional space as well.

Peter Lancto and I were performing constantly at the university and we had many private engagements as well; I was still on the faculty at the Boston Conservatory and my life with my piano continued beautifully, sometimes at a rapid pace, sometimes slowly but all in all life was good. Peter was my soul mate by this time and we relied on each other a great deal. I found that friends like Peter were far and few between.

Mary McLaughlin walked into my life and gave it a twist I never thought would happen. She was a music student from Ballenasloe, Ireland who had written the

Conservatory desiring to study music for the summer. The Conservatory admitted her and when she arrived they assigned her to me. It has always been my belief that there are no coincidences in life and this was to be another example of that conviction.

Mary was a delightful human with a very full head of dark, dark hair and pure white skin so typical of those from the Misty Isles. She was average in height and had a sort of solid, stocky build and came forth with the most wonderful brogue you ever heard. I could sit and listen to her talk for hours.

Her music skills were marginal but through her lessons we gradually learned all about each other and we liked each other immediately. She told me that the Irish were somewhat of a fatalistic people with dark, brooding personalities from time to time, probably due to the continual overcast skies and interminable rain. The Irish are a strong-willed, determined people who never passed up a friendship or a glass of good whiskey. Mary told me all about herself and I did so with her. She didn't have a great deal of money and at one point I offered to have her come stay with me and I was so glad when she accepted. Her boyfriend in Ireland was continually after her to come home and get married and she was desperately homesick for him and Ireland. I talked to her about hanging in and finishing the summer and I'm quite sure that if it hadn't been for me she would have given up and gone home.

I told her all about Jean Francois and Laurie and how I had met them on the voyage to Europe and of the wonderful love affair in Paris. To my surprise Mary said she wanted to help me reconnect with both Jean Francois and Laurie. We put our heads together and came up with a scheme to contact Laure who could be our private investigator since I couldn't contact Jean Francois at home or at work. I didn't even know if he was married or not. I had lost all contact. I wrote to

Laure at her last known address asking her to see what had become of Jean Francois. One day the letter arrived and I must confess my hand was trembling a bit as I tore open the envelope. The letter was from Madame Chivot herself because as she explained, Jean Francois had told her all about me. She felt she could contact me directly because of all I had been to her husband. I read on afraid of what was to follow. The news was as if my heart was torn from my chest when she wrote that Jean Francois had died of a massive heart attack at age forty five. The events of our time together in France whirred through my head like a kaleidoscope and the love and emotion swelled through my whole body and brought uncontrollable tears. Mary was there for me and held me like a child until the hurt eased up and I could regain composure. The love of my life was gone and there was a gaping hole in my existence.

Some time later, Mary, who was a scrappy little thing who wouldn't let go of a challenge, got me to agree to find Laurie. Mary called Kings College, his alma mater and was connected to the registrar's office who gave us the last known address of Mr. Laurie Stephen Phillips. I wrote him a short note telling him about Jean Francois' death and asked him to contact me by phone. It wasn't long before Laurie called expressing his regrets about Jean Francois and his pleasure that I was well and consumed by my piano. I told him about Mary and that it was conceivable that I would be coming to Europe for Mary's wedding in the fall. He sounded truly excited and said that we would surely see each other if I did make the trip.

I couldn't bear the pain of Jean Francois. He would always be in my heart and I would never lose the love I had for him and I needed balance so the pain would not keep coming back. By contacting Laurie I felt that a new relationship would help keep Jean Francois from bubbling back to the surface. Maybe I could replace that lost feeling, that emptiness with new life. We started to correspond but we also made many, many phone calls; I to him and he to me. It was his voice, his accent, his way with words that kindled my interest and I knew I was going to Ireland.

I didn't know just how soon I was to go to Ireland because it wasn't but a few weeks later that Mary, in all her exuberance, came to me and announced that she and her boyfriend Geoff were to be married in August, soon after she finished her studies. Mary's eyes sparkled as she invited me to be a part of her life by attending the wedding. I accepted on the spot and started mentally planning the trip.

This had to be worth the time and money so I planned to spend as much time as possible as I had never traveled the British Isles. Laurie was delighted when I told him and we looked at calendars and charted a course that would begin in Ireland where I would visit Mary and spend a week or more with her. Laurie would join me for the wedding and then we would return to England and he would take it from there. Tickets were bought, wardrobe was bought, luggage was bought and time stood still while I anticipated my departure. My piano was the love of my life but it couldn't go out to dinner, it couldn't dry the dishes and it couldn't go to bed with me. If there was any chance of recreating what I had with Jean Francois, I wanted to take it. I wanted a new love in my life and Laurie was waiting for me and I was eager to see him. Aer Lingus here I come and maybe this would be the turning point in my life I was looking for; just maybe.

Chapter 13

Do these things float? I wondered to myself as the jumbo jet lifted off the runway at Boston's Logan Airport. I had only one prior flying experience but it was short and over land. All there was below me on this flight was water and I was as nervous as I was excited to be going. Everything was left behind me and I needed to get away. I wasn't even going to miss Baby on this trip. Goodbye mother, goodbye family, goodbye Dorchester; I was on my way and there was nothing nor anyone who could interfere with my turning this new page in my life.

The priest sitting next to me was elderly and what hair he had left was gray. He broke the ice by asking where I was going and I marveled at his accent. I have always been aware of accents and I have a good ear for them and when he spoke with a very pronounced brogue, I was amused and wanted to try to talk that way myself.

We engaged in wonderful conversation and it made the time fly by. He wanted to know all about my music career and I wanted to know all about the religious strife ongoing in Ireland. He told me how the religious differences and the anger and hatred were being passed on from generation to generation and if it didn't stop, the violence would never cease. He was very concerned about it and I gathered that he was quite high up in the church hierarchy.

We flew over the coast of Ireland on the way to Shannon Airport and I looked down upon this grand patchwork quilt of green. Not just green but many, many greens bordered by walled fences of rock. No wonder they call Ireland the Emerald Isle. The passengers were all excited and moving around so they could see the land below and as I listened to all the buzzing conversation I realized how many different accents there were. This was truly an international flight and soon to end as the captain announced our descent into Shannon.

Packing for a two month trip requires that I put my house in the luggage. I don't know why it is but I just seem to think I will need everything I own including the kitchen sink. We deplaned and went to the carousels where the luggage emerged from the bowels of the airport thrown by unseen hands onto a conveyor. Not thrown in my case but rather heaved onto the conveyor. My four bulging bags came up rather quickly and it was all I could do to hoist them off the carousel. I went to get a cart, a big cart, and put the bags onto it when the fleeting thought came to mind that what I really needed was a forklift.

I approached the Customs counter and the agent's eyes grew wide with fear as he saw this rumpled little black lady with four behemoth bags approaching. It took me and him to get the bags on the counter and he rolled his eyes when he lifted his end. I had nothing to fear about customs but it is funny how it is a nervous time because someone is looking through your belongings, underwear and all.

The agent continued to roll his eyes finishing my last bag when I glanced over to the gate and there was Mary yelling out my name and waving her hands like a cheerleader. Next to her was this little man who was built like a stick and shorter than Mary by a couple of inches. He was as pale as milk and as skinny as Ichabod Crane. Then I realized, "My god, this is Geoff." After Mary and I exchanged hugs, I got a hug from Geoff as well and he was very kind in welcoming me to Ireland.

Mary and her people were wonderful to me for the next weeks taking me all over the countryside and showing me the sights of the area including a beautiful quarry where a startling green rock was mined. We toured the peat bogs and walked the villages. The family had an upright piano so I played frequently for them and we had very good conversation in the evenings. Geoff would pop in and out during the week and it was very apparent that he and Mary were truly in love. All in all it was a nice time.

The ferry from Liverpool arrived in Dublin where we had arrived an hour early. I was full of anticipation since I hadn't seen Laurie in such a long time. But you can't miss Laurie. He is quite tall and he had blondish hair and eyeglasses as thick as Coke bottles and when he came through the gate I was on my feet and running to him as he put his bag down and threw his arms around me in a big hug. It was a warm reunion and after introductions all around, we jumped into the car returning to Ballinasloe chattering all the way.

The contrast between Mary's wedding and Velicia's was dramatic. The beautiful formality of Velicia's with her gorgeous, hand made gown, the tuxedos, flowers, huge church were typically American. However, Mary's wedding was marvelously stark simplicity. It was held in a classic Irish, cottage-like Catholic church; very small, made of whitewashed rock and situated on a hillside grove of trees. The blushing bride wore her hair in a bun behind her head and a common gray suit and the beaming groom, in black. They were a beautiful young couple. The alter was not ornate and the priest wore his fine vestments of white over his black frock. The wedding was attended only by family, Laurie and me. There couldn't have been a dozen people there but the ceremony was very spiritual and quiet; not at all like the flamboyant display so often performed in our country.

We bade farewell to the bride and groom and Laurie rented a car for us and we drove south and west to the shore. We rented a very quaint cottage in County Clair overlooking the islands off shore. We loved it when, on the first morning, a cow stuck its head through our kitchen window and we had breakfast with the cows. We needed the time because Laurie had promised to help me complete my master's degree thesis. He was experienced in thesis writing since he had completed both his masters and his PhD. We put in long hours on my thesis and Laurie's way with words, his charm and intellect were making the fairy tale come alive again. He loved what he loved about me and I loved about him what I loved. It wasn't the same as Jean Francois but love nevertheless. This was my life, my fairy tale and Laurie was who I had to make it work. Those were sweet days where we worked some, took long walks and made love. Laurie had a wonderful joie d' vivre and would point out all the beautiful things and beautiful people we would encounter. He was a magnet to people, no matter where we were. We would go to a pub and people would gather around us to hear his stories and jokes.

It was on one of those long walks on a bright, sparkling day where the sun shimmered off the sea as it fell into the evening, that Laurie proposed to me. He stopped, casually reached into his pocket and took out a ring, which he said had been his mother's. Whenever Laurie tried to be romantic, he would blush, and blush he did. The ring was absolutely gorgeous. It had four nice sized diamonds across and the setting was European gold, eighteen or twenty carat and the scrollwork was elaborate with perfect workmanship He put the ring on my finger and asked me to marry him....and I said, "Yes."

Now it was time for planning. Laurie was a planner and so was I. First, we had to get me graduated. Next. Laurie had to get his two businesses straightened out as to what he wanted to do with them. Would he sell them both and move to America or would he just sell one and go back and forth from England to America. These were immediate things that needed to be resolved but at least there seemed to be a future for me; a bright future I thought.

The ferry to Liverpool was right on schedule after we bade farewell to County Clair. Laurie and I jumped into his car and we drove north to the Yorks where he needed to move his things from his apartment. The company he worked for had closed down after losing government funding and the employees had been given severance pay. Laurie had taken his severance package and invested in two sporting goods stores; one in Lowestoft on England's east coast and the other shop was in the same area within a short drive.

We drove the long drive to Yorkshire and picked up his belongings as planned and now we were able to spend a great deal of time truly getting to know each other. Most of it was good sharing but there were a few warning signs that I either didn't notice or maybe I refused to notice. I wanted love in the worst way and here was Laurie, an educated man, a capable man and we had a connection that dated back to when I was a young girl. It was a fairy story I wanted to be true. Despite all, I wanted it to be true.

We headed southeast to Lowestoft where we dropped off his things in his new apartment, which was right over his sporting goods store. We spent a few days planning a trip to Paris and I placed a call to Laure who was very excited to see us. We would catch a ferry in Felixstowe to cross the North Sea to Zeebrugge in Belgium. Then we would drive the short distance to Paris. The weather had been grand and I was silent taking it all in. I was so excited to return to the place where all had begun. It was a coming home.

Laure greeted me with all the enthusiasm I remembered declaring that I hadn't changed at all. She called me "fou ma petite", her little crazy one. And we started the natural recollection of times past and we laughed and chattered away. I had introduced her to Laurie to whom she took an immediate dislike, and he, not being the center of attention, which he required at all times, became immediately jealous. We continued our memories and Laurie would make sly remarks about anything, poking fun at our girl-like banter. Laure didn't like English men to begin with but Laurie had struck a bone. It was out and out silent warfare. When we were alone she said, "Jacqui, you cannot marry this man! He does not understand you at all." I, of course, defended him and proclaimed his accolades. The fairy story had to be true!

We were on a tight time frame and we could only spend a couple of days in Paris. Laure showed us around a little bit but things were not good between the two of them and I wanted to get away quickly. She warned me again saying that Laurie was not Jean Francois, which of course I knew but stubbornly refused to admit. Laure kissed me goodbye, nothing could ever come between us as friends but Laurie was as close as anyone or anything to doing just that. We retraced our steps and went back to Lowestoft to gather my things. The days before leaving for Liverpool on the way home were growing long. The gild was off the Lilly and all the warning signs became more evident and after a few days I was ready to go home. I desperately needed my piano. I had had enough but not enough to admit.

The trip to Liverpool might as well have been to Moscow. It was agonizingly long and not much was said. Laurie's way of handling things was to pretend they never happened. He believed that if you just ignore the problem, it would work itself out. There have never been two people who ignored reality as much as we did. When we reached the ferry terminal, he simply said that we would write and call frequently. He was to try to sell one of his businesses and then go across the Pond and look around the States to see if there was something he could do there. There was an empty kiss goodbye like all the other kisses I had received from him, and with a wave of the hand I boarded the boat. I was a wreck but now that I was free of him, a huge load was off my shoulders. I went on board and breathed the clean salt air and enjoyed being happier than I had been in weeks.

The train back to Ballinasloe was a short and pretty ride. Mary met me at the station and I spent the next several days relaxing and playing the piano. She and Goeff had just come back from a brief honeymoon and she was very happy. We talked about her students and I introduced her to one piano-four hands, which she thoroughly enjoyed. I was enjoying my freedom and I slept well each night. I was homesick but when it was time to go to the airport I wished I could have stayed longer. Mary was special and we agreed that she and Goeff must come to America some day.

Goodbyes to Mary and Goeff with smiles and tears, and this time I was all alone in the airplane seat for which I was very thankful. I needed to be alone with my thoughts without small talk with neighbors. I recalled the last few weeks wondering whether it was going to work. Was I doing the right thing? I looked down at that beautiful ring on my finger and it drew me back to the fairy tale. I would be OK and being engaged put me one up on my mother. Velicia was going to be ecstatic. She had talked with Laurie many times and he had sent her presents on several occasions. And as I was drifting off, that inner voice, that part of our soul that talks to us, asked me over and over, "Are you sure?" I didn't know how to answer but I did know that when that plane landed, I was home.

Chapter 14

Dorchester hadn't changed a bit but I had. I found everyone the same and healthy and Baby had never looked better. I was sporting my ring, my thesis was complete and I had accomplished everything I had set out to do. I was a new person. It had been a long time since I had been able to get away for any length of time and it felt good. Most of all, I wasn't so much my mother's daughter; I was a woman with her in the same house.

Velicia was very pleased at my engagement and expressed how much she liked Laurie. He was always kind and fun loving with her on the phone; kidding her and making her laugh. He had charmed her ever since I had rediscovered him and she loved it. Willie even accepted the fact and didn't make much of a fuss but I knew that when the happy face rubbed off she would revert to her old nasty self. But for now things were good.

All the while Laurie and I were on the phone with each other. I continually quizzed him as to how the sale of his businesses was going and it was very frustrating. He would talk on and on and at the end of the conversation I knew nothing more than at the beginning. The deal was that he was to sell the business and then we were to be married in America. It wasn't happening. Something inside of me knew that it never would but we kept on keeping the illusion alive....just in case. I was engaged, I had the ring but my energy was focused on my piano; the one thing in life I could undeniably rely upon.

I am convinced that God sends certain people into our lives and for good reason. One of the major plans that Laurie and I had made was that, if he could sell one of the businesses, we could live in Lowestoft for half the year and Maine the other half. We selected Maine because it is on the same latitude as Lowestoft and the climates were very similar; cool, moist and on the ocean. I was teaching a woman named Margaret Crowley who had studied the piano as a girl and decided as an adult to resume the piano. Her roommate was a Cathy Martin who also expressed interest in the piano. As a result I had found two adult students, which was a refreshing change from the children of the Boston public school system. They were both pleasant women and we got along very well.

Cathy was telling me that she was teaching art in Plymouth and living in Jamaica Plain but that she owned a home in Kittery, Maine where she lived with her sister in the summer. The more we got to know each other the more she kept inviting me to visit in Maine. One day Cathy informed me that she and her sister, Brenda, were hoping to have me give a concert in their house. I agreed. The big day arrived and Cathy picked me up and drove the fifty miles to Kittery. The house was not large, just a two bedroom ranch style that had a small den off the living room. The piano was in the den and the attendees were seated around the living room on sofas and folding chairs. It was a beautiful day and the windows were wide open allowing the air to drift in and my music to drift out. It was a wonderful time and the small audience was very appreciative.

When the concert was over, Cathy suggested that I plan to come up and start teaching a day a week and since Cathy was already a student she felt certain that more people could be found to make it worth my while. This arrangement led to a most remarkable relationship. I would come up and teach on a Thursday, stay the night and return the next morning. Brenda would drive me on her way to work to the bus terminal in Portsmouth, New Hampshire, right across the river from

Kittery. It was a nice arrangement but the relationship with Brenda was becoming much more than that; it was becoming a very meaningful friendship.

The summer flew by as they do and it was time for Cathy to return to Jamaica Plain and start school. It was then that Brenda and I were able to spend significant time with each other. The more we got to know each other, the more we realized how much alike we were. I would take the bus from Boston early on a Thursday and arrive in Portsmouth whereupon I would walk across the Memorial Bridge to Kittery, then a short walk to the house past a little market where I would stop and buy my bottle of wine, then past the baseball field to Cathy and Brenda's house. I would teach all day and when five thirty arrived, Brenda would come crashing through the door, throw her coat on the sofa, holler hello to me and pour us both a glass of wine. We would catch each other up on the events of the day and our lives. We became good friends and I realized how special she was.

Maine was a wonderful addition to my life. I was dealing with people I really liked and who had an intellect that stirred my own. It allowed me to get out of Boston and the stagnation of my negative household. I learned to do things I had never done before; like figuring out how to take a bus out of Boston to Portsmouth, New Hampshire. It was a new venue, a new stage and it was very refreshing. Adding Kittery to my life meant that something had to go and there was no question in my mind that it was going to be the Boston Conservatory. Twenty-six years of teaching there and still "Adjunct Faculty" led me to turn in my resignation and the Dean replied that he was sorry that I was leaving but you would think that there would be some sort of farewell event. Nothing! It was as though I had never been there.

I remember that when I walked from the Conservatory to Boylston Street and took that familiar turn that it would be the last time after all those years. It is part of my psyche that when something as painful as this happens, I don't fully feel the pain until later. The full realization seeps in little by little by little. It seems like there is something inside of me that says if you feed it to me little by little I can survive. And that is what happened when the full realization hit me I was off and running into something else. I don't like to remember pain and that is why I am able to keep going.

I returned to Baby and poured myself into her as though I was cleansing myself of the hurt. I was playing more with Peter. Peter, my mentor, my friend, my compatriot who gave me the encouragement I needed to build my self-esteem. That big man who could fill a doorway was as gentle and compassionate as he could be to remind me of my talent and that any setback means nothing because I can overcome it. We played more and more together and just when I thought it was all back together, it happened. Why do I have to lose the ones I love so much? First Jean Francois and now my wonderful Peter. Just thirty-nine years old and dead from a rapid moving cancer. My Peter, as big as a house and as kind and good a man as there ever was. I received the news from his parents and just cried, I cried for days. Why do the good die so young? What will I ever do without Peter? All the questions in the world would not bring him back but I will hear his music forever. I went to that funeral on a cold and wet Boston day and his whole music world was there; his friends all played his favorite tunes and everyone told good stories about a good person. Goodbye Peter, I will play for you too.

Would it ever stop; there was more pain to come as I learned that Fontaine was very ill. Soon afterward he passed away and it was a funeral I also attended because despite his drinking and lack of household support, he was a kind and gentle creature who was, in the early days, a daddy figure for me. I think he would have really been something had my mother not degraded and berated him the way she did. Fontaine was gone and I was sad that he was.

Velicia and Petey announced that he was going to be transferred to Washington, D.C. What a surprise. He thought it was a great move in his career. He had to stay with this job and he wasn't about to give it up. Velicia liked the thought of warmer weather and with three children it was going to be better for all of them. Particularly when the move would take them away from his mother who was at the root of any problems they had in the marriage. I was happy for her and gave her a grand send off. Her moving left me and Willie at home alone and we coexisted as best we could. I was busy with my life and she was busy criticizing it.

Velicia had been gone for about a year and as time went on Willie and I started to clash on almost a daily basis. My mother was once again making my life miserable. At the same time I received a distress call from Velicia saying that Petey had driven the family into destitution and she couldn't take it any more. Their relationship had fallen apart and her marriage was truly in trouble. She knew she had to leave Petey and the house. She had a friend who knew the situation and told her to move to Hampton, Virginia where she could take advantage of the system and get a place to live while she reestablished herself. It was public living and not very comfortable. She was ashamed as to where her life had led her. Velicia is a very proud person but at that time her pride was shot and she was as low as I had ever seen her. But at least she was away from the fear and pain that Petey had caused. That is when I made the decision. I told Velicia that I was going to sell the house and move to Virginia so I could help her. She agreed.

I spoke to Laurie and told him about the problems that Velicia was having and that I was going to move to Virginia to help. I knew he would agree with my decision for a couple of reasons; one was that he loved Velicia and always spoke so highly of their conversations and, two, he knew he hadn't done anything to make our marriage possible. The sale of his business was still a mystery and he was too busy manipulating people to pressure me to return to England. In a way, we were both relieved that there was another major issue in our lives that kept our marriage in the future where it belonged.

I told Willie my plans and she went berserk telling me that even though her name wasn't on the deed she had lived in that house for over twenty five years and there was no way I could sell the house from under her. I told her to "watch my smoke" and immediately called a realtor who told me how to price it and put a sign out in front. As life and my music would have it I mentioned to a student that the house was for sale and she surprised the hell out of me by saying she wanted to buy it....and she did. It was that quick, that easy and that is why I knew that things were meant to be. Mother had contacted some attorney and sent him to my door one night telling me all sorts of legal mumbo jumbo about not selling the house because I would be served papers if I did. That scared the shit out of me so I contacted another student and asked if she knew an attorney. She knew just the person. That is how my life works, through my music. It always comes through to help in times of trouble. I called the attorney named Carolyn LaMar and told her the situation and she came to see me. She handed me some of her cards and simply said that if anyone called, give them her name and number or if anyone comes to the house again, give them her card. Under no circumstances was I to talk to anyone, particularly my mother. Carolyn would represent me in all discussions. This woman was sharp and we started an attorney/client relationship that was to last many years

There is no venom like the venom spewed at me by my mother as we both packed up to leave the house. She walked the neighborhood telling everyone what a horrible person I was to sell her house from under her. We didn't say three words to each other as we went about the task of the move. I packed all my things myself, gave away a good deal of furniture that Velicia couldn't use and made arrangements for Baby to be shipped to Virginia. It was a crazy time but I was a woman on a mission and if Willie wanted to deal with me she had to do it through my attorney.

The closing of the house met some snags and I was petrified that I would have to spend more time in the house with Willie. I told Carolyn and she told me to get out of the house and get my ass down to Virginia and that she would take care of all the final details. All I had to do eventually was to sign the papers. Carolyn handled the closing, my mother, my mother's attorney and even sat on the stoop and waited for the movers to arrive and load my things. She was, and is, a saint. Thank God for her.

I left the house so early in the morning there was no hint of dawn. It was more like an escape than a leaving. I was free and there was a certain all encompassing sense of adventure as I boarded the train headed for Newport News, Virginia. My mission was clear and I had fled the bondage of my own mother; a very unnatural realization.

Velicia and the children met me at the station and we hugged and "ooohd" and "aaahd" about the kids and then jumped into the car and went directly to the apartment where Velicia had made room for me. I was hopeful I would have a good impact on her and the children. My work was cut out for me. All the things I didn't do when she was young came back to confront me now that she was an adult. She had been raised by my mother while I was making a living and Velicia was an interesting mixture of my mother and me. The next three years were to be ones of establishing myself as mother and grandmother, being a part of the household dealing with discipline and instruction for the children, providing basic orderliness and organization, all the while knowing that I was a guest in the house; a difficult role at best. At least it freed up Velicia to go to work each day and slowly reconstruct her self esteem; and that she did. She had a position training people in electronic communications and with her personality, she performed quite well in that scenario. She also had struck up a new relationship with a bright young man who was to be very influential in her life. All in all I was doing what I had come to do.

I'm sure it has happened to many people but I woke up one morning and asked myself to face the facts of my existence. Above all I wanted to play my piano again, I wanted to teach again, I wanted to be independent again and I would have given anything to have a man in my life again. I realized that I couldn't do any of these things in Virginia. I didn't want to stay in a ninety nine percent black community, which had no, or very little, appreciation for classical music. I wanted it the way it used to be surrounded by Caucasians, who had an appreciation of what I do and of European culture. I couldn't see myself going to the Baptist church every Sunday and singing in the choir, cooking for the church supper and trying to teach little black kids how to play a piano they didn't want to learn. I needed a change.

Wouldn't you know Willie was still in my life. She had been in contact with Carolyn through her attorney charging that I owed her money because I had been supporting her for so many years; now claiming that I should continue. The attorneys talked and Carolyn told me that she would offer a certain amount and that if they didn't accept it we would go to court. I told her that was fine but I had another issue where I needed help. My passport had expired and I needed help in obtaining another. I had never been able to find a document confirming my birth but Carolyn, my legal buzz saw persisted and found my birth certificate in Florida. She explained that when I was born the midwife documented my birth in one county but filed it in another where she lived. That solved the mystery of never having had a birth certificate.

Where was I in life? I couldn't go back to Dorchester where my mother would pursue and pillage me at any opportunity. I couldn't stay in Virginia where my welcome was starting to wear out and I didn't have the where with all to go somewhere else and start all over. As a result I picked up the phone and with great trepidation called Mr. Lawrence Stephen Phillips and said that I was coming to England and we had to determine where our relationship was going. At first he didn't believe me, then he made a joke of it but then he realized that I was serious and he became very optimistic and turned on the charm as only Laurie could. He mentioned how we would make it and that together we would be a real team. He told me he had bought a cottage right around the corner from his shop and said that I would love it. This rosy picture confirmed the fact that I was on my way to Lowestoft.

Carolyn again went to work and developed all the paperwork that was required for a United States citizen to travel to England for the purpose of marriage, which required extended stay. This all took time and while the process was progressing I was in touch with my friends in Dorchester and Maine; primarily Brenda who, herself, was in a new marriage to her husband, Bob. I told her what was happening and she extended her total support and said if there was anything she could do to help, they were there for me. With this support I was off and running and my fairy tale imagination had total control.

One of the people I contacted was a former student, Keith Witherell, who had become not only a student, but a friend. He made arrangements for Baby to stay in a private home in Cape Elizabeth, Maine, right outside of Portland. The oldest son was taking lessons and although I didn't like the idea of someone else playing her, at this time in my progress I had no choice. At least I knew she was safe. I thanked Keith profusely not knowing how significant he would be in my future like so many other people who entered my life because of her. This is the real significance of my piano, my Baby, the instrument of my existence. How many times had she led me to the circumstances, the places, and the people who wove the fabric of my being. It is as though my piano and the music from her were real beings who, like guardian angels, guided and protected me through the turmoil I had created for myself. Sometimes when I caressed her keys I almost could hear her talk to me; sometimes comforting me; sometimes chastising me; sometimes laughing at me but always protecting me. It was so hard to leave her. I felt very vulnerable but I was committed because the fairy tale was much prettier, much more attractive and tempting than the pain of my reality.

I am ready to go. The paperwork was complete, I was packed, I had my passport, Laurie was waiting and I was to depart Boston Logan Airport in three days. I arrived in Round Pond, Maine to stay with Brenda and her husband who were to drive me to the airport. We had a wonderful three days and I was able to verbalize all that was going through my chaotic mind. Brenda and Bob were very receptive and wanted to know all about Laurie and my new life. I kept up the positive façade as best I could and when I told them of my great expectations I knew I was impressing them while convincing me. The more I talked, the more they were impressed and the more I was convinced. It is wonderful what the human mind can do. It can make fairy tales come true; it can make the uncomfortable, comfortable; it can make ugly people beautiful; it can make wrong, right. But I didn't know that, I believed every word I said. The three days passed quickly when we loaded my gargantuan bags into the SUV and off we went to Boston. Well, I said, "Here I go."

Chapter 15

Gatwick Airport appeared on the horizon after a non-descript flight overnight. The people deplaned and we had to go through customs, which was a typically scary event for the agent checking me through. I put my bags on a cart and walked with anticipation to the waiting area. The throng was large but I picked him out immediately. He was easy to pick out all right but not for good reasons He looked awful. He is tall to begin with but he looked oh so tired; he had aged a great deal since I had seen him last. He had large bags under his eyes, his hair was disheveled as were his clothing. He was not neatly attired at all and he smiled a somewhat embarrassed smile. This was not the Laurie I had last seen. It was as though he was hesitant to be there. I, of course, ignored all this and went to him, gave him a kiss and he hugged me back. It was strange but it was as though I was meeting someone for the first time. We jumped into the car and started the long trek to Lowestoft in almost complete silence. Everything was subdued and quiet. We stopped for coffee and the conversation was about everything except us; it was about the passing scenery; the various towns and what they were noted for; the events of the day, week, year; anything of any interest.... except us.

We arrived at Lowestoft and Laurie drove to his street but we couldn't just drive to the "cottage," we had to stop at a neighbor's house to drop my bags off and walk to the rear entrance. We approached the building and my heart slumped at the sight. All around the backdoor yard was debris that had been torn out of the house and just discarded in heaps. Lumber, plumbing, wallboard, an old stove and a barrel which, God knows contained what. He took me inside and as we walked in we were confronted with an old rusty hot water heater, which we had to step around in order to enter the house. One of the first things I saw was a bathroom with no door. The toilet looked as though it was over a hole, not on plumbing pipe. I would not touch the sink. I don't think it was ever cleaned and it was dirt, not just dust but black dirt that was caked over the porcelain. Then Laurie took me to the next room, the kitchen, where there was a sink, a stove and a refrigerator all in a row, galley style and the kitchen led to the living room, which was a frightening sight. The floors throughout the entire dwelling were concrete with the exception of a carpet in the living room that was a dark print with holes in it and which I suspected had been pissed on. The "cottage" was below street level and when you looked out the windows all you could see were feet walking by, so not very light at all. But all around the room were box upon box of junk. Absolutely worthless, good for nothing junk. He explained that he went to a number of "boot sales" which were like yard sales but things were sold out of the trunk or "boot" of a car. The problem was that if you saw one thing you wanted, you had to buy the whole box whether you wanted the items or not. The bigger problem was (I learned much later) that Laurie had a compulsion, a mental disorder that prevented him from throwing anything out. His brother suffered from it and so had his father so it seemed genetic in nature. Other than the boxes, there were two stuffed chairs that were so dirty I wouldn't sit in them and a meager table or two. He had said that he was buying a new sofa and chair but there was no evidence of that, it was appalling.

I froze. I literally froze at the specter of what I had done. I had made the biggest mistake of my life. The mistake became bigger when he showed me the upstairs and the bedroom. I would never lie down on those sheets, on that filth. Thank heavens I had some sheets in my bags but when we went to bed I couldn't let him touch me. He hadn't bathed in God knows how long and he smelled horribly. I curled up on one corner of the bed and virtually cried myself to sleep. Oh my God, what have I done?

Despite these horrible surroundings we unbelievably went about planning the wedding. I was numb, I was in a fog but I had committed to all this and everything was on a one-way ticket. I had enough money to get there but there wasn't enough to get back….I had no options. I had gone through so much shit to get here I was not about to go back and have people point fingers at me and say," I told you so." I refused to be humiliated in that fashion and I am just that stubborn that I thought maybe I could make a difference. When I knew Laurie in the past, he wasn't like this. Maybe living alone for so long does terrible things to people and I thought without any rational reason that I could help him and change what I saw. I had told Laurie that I was going to marry him and for some sick reason I felt obligated to carry it out. Jean Francois was dead and I had foolishly transferred all of the things I wanted in a man into Laurie. My imagination, my fairy tale had to be true; I had staked everything upon it. Oh my God, Baby where are you? If I could only play and play and play it would be all right but instead it was decided that we were to be married in Winchester, which was south of London, because a great many of Laurie's family lived in that area.

The trip to Winchester in Laurie's car was once again long and arduous. I was getting sick from fumes from the engine because there was a floor plate missing allowing the fumes to rise. I actually threw up and had a horrible headache from it all. I managed to pull myself together as we arrived but to this day I don't know how. The small entourage was assembled, not over twelve or fifteen people gathered at one of Laurie's relative's house. What a contrast! It was a beautifully manicured home with rock and flower gardens everywhere. The interior was immaculately kept with nothing out of place and the entire home sparkled with elegance. All in attendance were very kind to me and although I picked up on some raised eyebrows, the mood was light and friendly.

We had all the prearranged paperwork and all went to the church for the ceremony. The minister was a woman, a very pleasant person whom I immediately liked. I believe she was called a Vicar or something. She conducted a very nice ceremony and afterward, amongst all the "good lucks" and the "here here's" we went to the reception hall not far from the church where the liquor flowed and the speeches began. It was kind of a good-natured roasting with memories of Laurie in various circumstances throughout his life that were quite humorous. Nothing was said about me, of course, because nobody knew anything about me.

Following the wedding we drove south to the White Cliffs of Dover, which I had seen so many times on TV and in the movies. I wanted to see them. We drove to the observation area and I got out of the fumemobile and walked briskly to the edge. Laurie was panic stricken and I soon realized he had an extreme fear of heights so our stay was very brief and we climbed back into that horrible automobile and drove all the way back to Lowestoft to that horrible house of chaos and dirt. that he do something about putting a door on the bathroom. His response was to tack an old quilt over the doorway and I knew as I looked at that miserable answer to a real problem that I was doomed. I immediately started to hedge my existence by saying to myself that I could go it alone. I could start teaching and do it on my own.

I had met a lady who lived just down the street who had a piano and allowed me to play from time to time. When I explained my circumstances she told me that she

Mr. and Mrs. Laurie Phillips

had an apartment that was vacant and suggested that I move in and I could teach piano from her house. Laurie refused because it would have been money coming out of his pocket and he wasn't about to deal with that. As a result his answer to the problem was that we should go out and buy a piano so that I could teach from our house. We went to the suburbs and found a place that repaired uprights and spinets. I selected one that was remotely acceptable and Laurie reluctantly bought it. It was to be delivered that day and when it came I experienced a most humiliating event. In order to get the piano into the living room, we had to move boxes of junk that had been stacked to the ceiling. Those boxes were added to the boxes in the hallway and the entire process would have been hilarious if it weren't so pathetic. I couldn't stand it, I went upstairs to the bedroom and hid.

I looked at that miserable piano in that miserable house and I wanted to cry. I had thought that with a piano, things would be all right. The fairy tale would materialize and the piano would make all the rest of it all right. But it didn't happen and I slipped into a deeper depression than I endured before. I couldn't bring students in here; students of any kind, child or adult. I couldn't explain to any student as to why things looked as they did. I couldn't allow anyone to go to the bathroom through a quilt-covered doorway with a sink that was full of rust and crud of unimaginable origins. This was a den of iniquity and I don't know which was the stronger emotion, embarrassment or repulsion. None of anything made sense. I started to take more walks on the seashore. Laurie would spend all of his time secluded in his shop where we wouldn't have to deal with each other and I had to get out of the filth. I walked and walked looking at the clouds and the dark, angry North Sea. That ocean wasn't like the North Atlantic, it was a deep ominous blue and I'm not sure that these walks were helping or deepening my despair. I asked God to help me; I who hadn't really paid much attention to God in my life, although I knew He was there. I had always known He was there and I knew that my father was there too. I always knew that my father was looking out for his baby and if there was any consolation at that moment, it was that I wasn't as alone as I felt.

I decided that if I couldn't teach at our house, then maybe I could teach elsewhere. I found the woman who had offered her apartment as a studio and asked if I could teach in her house and much to my delight she said yes. It turned out that she wanted her grand daughter to take lessons and then decided that she would too. It was something to do, a little something, but Laurie just laughed and, as usual, made a joke of it. At that moment, that instant, with that smirk on his face, I realized just how much I disliked this man and how I disliked myself for getting into this macabre situation. Something had to happen.

Happen it did. I was at the piano one day waiting for a student when I looked up and thought there was a spider web, or a cobweb in front of my eyes. I tried to swipe it away but that didn't work. The image remained and I knew there was something wrong. It had happened before and I knew it was a vitreous hemorrhage; damage to rear of the eye causing shadows in vision. My doctor in Boston was excellent and repaired the tear in quadrants using laser. He had explained that repairing the whole lesion at once was too much for the eye at one time and could cause further damage. Several appointments in Boston and I was back to normal. Laurie and I made an appointment with the head of the Ocular Department at the Lowestoft Clinic called the Surgery. The doctor looked at my eyes and in a very cavalier fashion told me that there was nothing to worry about, they would repair it with laser surgery in one session. I told Laurie what my Boston surgeon had said and again he scoffed and made some remark about English doctors being every bit as good as American doctors would ever be. Now, I was not only miserable but also afraid. That night I sat down and wrote letters to Brenda, Jane Howard and attorney Carolyn explaining my plight. I couldn't admit what a horrible mistake I had made with Laurie so I used my eye condition as the reason for having to return quickly to the States for medical attention. They all read through the lines, however and I heard from each of them almost simultaneously. I received not only offers to help but with money from Brenda and an airline reservation from Jane.

I went home and started to pack. I told Laurie what was happening and he, again, made a joke of it. He exclaimed that he hoped I didn't think he was going to drive me to Gatwick because he was just too busy. Laurie hadn't been too busy doing anything since I had known him. I put the boxes outside in the walkway and told him that a man was going to come the next morning to take me to the airport. He laughed and went to bed saying he didn't think I could afford to go anywhere. Everything would be all right in the morning.

The cabbie was right on time and he helped me with the boxes and bags, which represented everything in the world I owned with exception of Baby. There were no goodbyes. Laurie was still in bed and as I looked out the back window of the moving cab at that dungeon of a house, there was an overwhelming feeling of good riddance; I didn't know whether to laugh or cry. My driver's name was Elton and he was very talkative which helped. He did not take the freeway to Gatwick but rather the back roads, which were the quintessential winding, hedge-lined rural roads of England. He was very interested in me and my situation and offered kind observations and condolences. I was surprised at how free I felt to talk about it with a total, cigarette-smoking stranger. It was the catharsis I needed to get it all out. The shame, the guilt, the loss were burdens I had to get rid of. How was I to face everyone at home? This would be an interesting homecoming to say the least.

Elton was wonderful, helping me not only by carrying my many bags and boxes but he actually came inside the terminal to make sure I was settled and comfortable. I tipped him well and thanked him profusely and waited for the departure. I was exhausted but I was going home! I had overcome another obstacle and I was to return and overcome one more repairing of my eyes. As I sat watching them prepare our airplane for departure, the conviction occurred to me that I was not returning to Boston nor certainly to Virginia; I was going to start this new chapter in Maine. It was a decision that was to alter my circuitous path through life....... permanently.

The plane, again, was uneventful and I had time to reflect upon all that had occurred bringing me to this point. It is horrible to think that a serious eye problem would be a blessing in disguise because it took the pressure of explaining my terrible judgment off my shoulders. The plane slammed down on the runway as my relationship with Laurie slammed down as well. I was home!

Jane Howard and her husband Alf met me at Logan and we drove to their house in Dorchester where they opened their home and their lives to me. Where, oh where would I be without these wonderful friends? I was home and I was safe; safer than I had been in months. I called Velicia immediately and when she answered she was bubbling over with excitement thinking I was still in England. When I explained about my eyes and that I was home for good, there was a long silence. She was obviously thinking that I was going to return to her house. I assured her that I was not but there was that void in our relationship on the phone that had always been there. It started with the fact that I was mentally and emotionally absent from her upbringing; Willie handled that, and Edward always blamed me for his not seeing her when we divorced, telling her that I wouldn't allow him to, when in reality, he was simply afraid I was going to ask him for money if he did....and that is true. Then, after spending the years with her in Virginia, neither she nor I were willing to repeat the experience. She had a new life, I knew that and I was heading for my own; the difference being I didn't know exactly where the hell I was going except that everything pointed to Maine.

Before I could go anywhere, however, I had to get attention for my eyes. I contacted Dr. Ross, my primary care physician at Massachusetts General and made an urgent appointment to see him. He took one look at me and referred me back to Dr. Di'Amico who had previously diagnosed vitreous hemorrhaging of the eyes due to diabetes. I knew the experience in England hadn't helped the condition at all. The next two months were spent going through numerous laser treatments of the eyes where little by little the condition was corrected. This treatment was in contrast to the 'do it all at once' approach in Lowestoft. Dr. Di'Amico and I became very well acquainted to say the least. There was no way I could teach with eyes in the condition they were upon my return and I knew I had to overcome the problem or my career would be over. Thank God for the Dr. Ross's and Di'Amico's of the world; the treatments worked.

During this period of time I was in touch with Keith and Jenny Witherell and they invited me to Portland one day to see Baby. My piano had been placed for safe keeping with friends of theirs in Cape Elizabeth, just south of Portland. It was a beautiful and large home with expansive, plush lawns and rock gardens and the people were very wealthy and very nice. We walked into the living room and there in the corner, in all of her glory, was my Baby. She was shined and polished and had never looked so good. Her top was up and she had been placed in a corner of the room on beautifully polished floors where whomever was playing could look out at the ocean through broad windows. I sat down immediately and ran my fingers over her keyboard and the urge to play and teach again was so strong, my heart palpitated with joy. I had to get to Maine!

Finally Dr. Di'Amico said that my eyes were good enough so that he didn't have to see me again but once every two or three months. With that news I contacted

Jenny who offered to start looking for an apartment for me in Portland. The call came and Jenny was excited that she had been able to locate some good prospects in good neighborhoods at reasonable rents. Brenda picked me up and we joined Jenny who had laid out an agenda of places to see. The three of us had a ball going from place to place evaluating the possibilities of not only good living arrangements but good teaching arrangements as well; not always an easy combination. It's amazing how you just know when something is right. We came upon this little apartment on Dean Street, just across from a schoolyard. It was on the first floor, which is a must and had an adequate living room for teaching and even a small waiting room just inside the door. Baby dominated the living room but it was adequate and all I could afford at the time. It was cozy and comfortable and now I had to furnish it. Just about everything I owned was either in Virginia in storage or in boxes at Brenda's house. God bless Keith, who not only moved Baby in for me but traveled all the way to Virginia and moved my furniture by rental truck. Brenda brought my warehouse full of clothing and I was in business.

The Jacqueline Gourdin Studio of Music sign was placed on the door and I started networking to attract all the students I could. Jenny was teaching at Thornton Academy, not far away, and arranged for a position as Adjunct Faculty teaching piano in their music department. After a few months of networking in the music world, I was introduced to a wonderful man, Dr. Eugene Corinci who was the Director of the Portland Conservatory of Music. After several interviews I was hired as Adjunct Faculty, which was perfect and filled up my schedule completely. Dr. Corinci was great to work with and he funneled students to me because he admired my method of teaching. Many of the other teachers weren't too happy about it when students were requesting me but Dr. Corinci handled it beautifully. We became good friends over the years and I owe much to him. I was up and running and truly happy. Thank you Daddy, you have done it again.

Chapter 16

Happy? Yes, but as I reminisce about all the situations I have overcome as I have fought through life, I never realized how it had affected my physical being. I have learned that we do all that we have to do to overcome obstacles and poisonous relationships but not without paying a price, a dear price.

It began right after I had left Edward; divorced Edward, and moved back to Dorchester with my mother that I realized I was having serious problems. My body temperature control was out of whack. One moment I was terribly hot and the next freezing. I thought, oh God, I'm going through menopause. Then, God, I'm too young for menopause. So I did what I had always done when things like this occurred, I ignored it. There came a time when I could no longer ignore the fact that there was a swelling under my chin on my throat. Also, I was having chest pains on my left side and finally Velicia demanded that I go and see a doctor.

Massachusetts General Hospital was a huge, formidable structure and as busy as any train station. I went to the front desk and took a seat for an interminable time until a doctor would see me. He took one look and sent me to the Endocrinology Department. The prognosis after several tests was Graves Disease, which is a malfunctioning of the thyroid gland. Holy shit, I had never had anything like that before....ever. They explained that it was a very serious disorder and that I was to have surgery. I said, "The hell I will," and they continued to tell me that surgery was the only treatment. I went on, in no uncertain terms, to tell them that I wasn't going to have surgery because I didn't have any insurance and they were not going to get paid. Then the eyebrows were raised. Then, and only then, did they tell me that there was an alternative treatment involving radioactive iodine?

Alternative?! This was something for a sci-fi movie. They put me in this special, heavy robe and put huge rubber gloves on my hands and took me to the basement of the hospital, away from all the other machinery and took me to this little machine that held a flask of something so clear that I couldn't tell there was anything in the glass. I was to put my gloved hands through two openings and take the glass in both hands and drink the contents. But before I did so, they all ran and hid behind a screen of some kind. The liquid was almost tasteless and because there wasn't any color at all, I wouldn't have known I was drinking anything except that I felt it go down my throat. I had to go back every day for several days so they could monitor how my body was tolerating the treatment. They did this with a damned Geiger Counter. I was clicking pretty well the first day but then the clicks slowed until there were none. It is amazing but that one shot of nuclear whatever did the job. The maintenance pill has to be taken for the rest of my life.....but, I am still here.

Chapter Two of the medical history was when I had left the Conservatory and was going to go to work for Lowell University while studying for my master's degree. They took me on as part and parcel of their Affirmative Action Plan to hire minorities but also because I had excellent credentials and background for their program. I filled two of the requirements of the AAP, I was female and I was black. Hallelujah! They also required that I take a physical examination for school records and it was then they discovered I was suffering from hypertension. All the stress of living with Willie plus all the changes in my life, plus the Graves Disease plus teaching private students, plus paying all the bills, plus ,plus, plus......all led up to hypertension. I found out that hypertension could reactivate the Graves Disease so I was placed on immediate medication including a diuretic for water retention and was advised about my diet. The pill drawer was starting to get full....but I am still here.

Dr. Ross is miniscule, one of the smallest men I have ever met. He walks on the balls of his feet in an almost musical fashion and speaks with the most under-toned voice. A very gentle soul who discovered Chapter Three of the Jacqueline Gourdin medical ensemble. Diabetes!!! I have goddamn diabetes? I couldn't believe it! I went home in a total state of disrepair and despair and told my mother who responded with her normal, kind, caring, sympathetic and observant; "Oh, its just a little sugar." I was sorry I told her anything at all.

I was to face a serious life changing events of my life. Everything I thought I knew about good health was soon to be challenged and changed. I had Diabetes II and I was assigned to a team at Mass. General where there was a team member for every aspect of managing the disease. One person would instruct me on how to take and record my blood readings, another was to prepare new diet menus, another was a physical therapist who taught the benefits of exercise and another who counseled me about the psychological impact of diabetes.

One of the major things I had to give up was my nightly reward of a drink of vodka. Over the years it had become my relaxer, my reward after a hard day. I never drank to excess but that one or two at the end of a day had become a habit I found rather hard to give up. I addressed the problem in the only manner I knew how...I quit cold turkey. I had to change a number of other things in my life as well but, oddly enough I wasn't taking diabetes too seriously. I already had two life-threatening diseases and, for some reason it was almost like, "Oh well, just something else to deal with." I wasn't cavalier about it, I just took it in stride. I would overcome this too. I now had my morning pills, my noon pills and my evening pills on top of the other pills. I had to find a bigger pill drawer…but I am still here.

I wasn't prepared for the next episode in the progress of this horrible disease, something I couldn't take in stride; my eyes started to go. Enter Massachusetts Eye and Ear Hospital, another medical institution with whom I would become intimately familiar. Dr. Di'Amico examined my eyes and informed me that I had a retina disorder due to the diabetes that could cause me to go blind. Oh, dear God, take away a foot, a leg but don't take away my eyes! Without my eyes, I lose my piano, I lose Baby, I will lose everything; I will lose my life.

I was with the best of the best. Dr. Di'Amico was the head of the Retinology Department and he explained what was going to happen. He started the treatments immediately to repair the damage to my retinas with laser surgery and that, hopefully, he could repair the damage or at least stop it from progressing further. I left that building a quaking, blubbering Jacqui Gourdin who had to walk back to the subway and take the long Red Line ride home, alone. Never had I felt so alone. Normally, when you have eye laser surgery, they want someone there to help you home. I had no one. I had no one who gave enough of a damn to be there with me when I needed them the most. I reached the "T" station and had to walk down the stairs with dark glasses on, holding onto the rail and then walk the ramp that led outside to Larchmont Street. I was half blinded by the surgery and the glasses; my legs were like jelly. But my spirits were more like jelly than anything because, for one of the first times I was facing my aloneness head-on. No rationalization - no excuses - no fairy tales - nothing. You are not supposed to cry after a laser treatment…but I did.

My doctors kept a good eye on me (no pun intended) but this goddamn disease is progressive. Now I was suffering from a condition called neuropathy, which compromises the vascular system. The extremities simply do not get enough blood and consequently always feel cold. But as long as my fingers were all right to play Baby, I would overcome anything they could throw at me. So, during all this I was teaching and even performing. I had to wear my special glasses and thick stockings but I could see well enough to read the music and that was all I needed. I found that my right eye was better than the left so I had to sit a little differently at the piano but I could see the music.

Dr. Di'Amico performed so many laser surgeries over the next two or three years I lost count but finally he exclaimed that I had stabilized and the treatments could stop for a while. The treatments, however, had caused a sloughing off of material that was in suspension in the fluid of the eye. Now, in addition to laser surgery, they had to remove the fluid from both eyes, cleanse the material from the fluid and return it to my eyes. Dr. Di'Amico first did one eye and then months later, the other. Now, however, it was time to address the problems with the front of my eyes. I had cataracts in both and he introduced me to his associate, Dr. Colby who was a specialist in cataract removal and lens replacement. She explained that she would remove one cataract that had grown over the lens and as a result, the lens had to be replaced as well. Once this was accomplished, there would be a substantial wait before correcting the other eye. The reason being that diabetes was progressive and could change things quickly. She had to be sure the first would be accepted by my body before doing the other.

The first operation was very successful. It was simply a matter of showing up, having the work done and then going home. The technology is incredible.

There was a period of about a year between the first operation and the second on the other eye. The second had such better results all stemming from the fact that the lens materials had improved so much in just that year. When the second eye was done I could read my music without having to enlarge the score.

Things started to get more stable. I needed no more surgeries but I had to be monitored very closely which meant that, even though I had moved to Maine, I had to see the doctors frequently for checkups and blood work. My piano is as good as ever, my student base has grown, I have been performing with Keith on a regular basis and other than having to take a ton of medication, my life has regained some semblance of normalcy.

Charlie lived next door to me on Dean Street. "Uncle Charlie" I called him. He resembled Tweedle Dee and Tweedle Dumb in 'Alice in Wonderland.' He was a very kind, Nebbish, sort of a man. I was telling him how I needed a larger apartment because Baby was not sounding very well in the confined quarters she was in. He brightened very suddenly and said that he had a friend that had a lovely apartment on Pitt Street; not far away and in a better neighborhood. The next thing I knew I was being driven by Uncle Charlie to see the place. I walked in after admiring the neighborhood and fell immediately in love. It was perfect; twice as much room, newly redecorated, bright and cheery with an extra bathroom for students off the kitchen hallway. The next thing I knew I was writing the rent deposit check. Everything went so smoothly, I knew God had his hand on one shoulder and my father had his hand on the other.

The three burly men came to move my Baby. Each was as big as a house and they brought in their apparatus for piano moving. I was amazed because that piano was dismantled, crated and moved to Pitt Street within an hour. I had demanded professionals but these guys were terrific. Again, I was in business and the Jacqueline Gourdin Studio of Music sign was on the door by that afternoon. The owners of the house were wonderful and became good friends who enjoy good music. Books unpacked, boxes finally thrown out, I settled into a nice rhythm of living.

I was cruising, for three years I enjoyed the fruits of my piano and Pitt Street. I was playing, performing, teaching and literally turning people away. Life was so good! All of a sudden I developed a case of what I thought was asthma. I would take some medication but it would come right back. I was having real respiratory problems but it was recital time of year and I was in great demand. And as usual the Jacqui Gourdin denial kicked in and I ignored it; shoved it under the carpet.

Under the carpet until the following Sunday when Jeffrey, my lovely trombone player and I were performing, I realized I had to see someone. I was gasping for breath and barely made it through the performance. My dear friend and business manager, Ellen Ryan and I went through the Yellow Pages and found a doctor in Scarborough who would see me. All my regular doctors were in Boston and there was no time to see them. Ellen drove me to the doctor's office who she gave me a cursory examination but said she couldn't do much until she saw an x-ray of my lungs. The x-ray office was two doors down in another office complex. Ellen drove me and let me off at the door because it had started to rain. I went into the vestibule while she was parking the car and I suddenly realized I was in real trouble. I tried to signal her through the window and she came running as I started to collapse. Dear reader, please understand why and how much I believe in a God because there were about three or four EMTs standing in the hallway who ran to me just as I was about to hit the floor. They put me on a gurney and the ambulance was waiting. If I was going to

Jeffrey, my glorious concert trombonist

collapse anywhere, it should have been right there.

They started to work on me right away with sirens blazing. They were trying to give me oxygen but I had it in my head that if they placed that mask over my nose and mouth I was going to die. Let me tell you, when you think you are going to die, you fight like hell, and that I did. It eventually took two to hold me down and the other to keep the damned mask over my mouth. Thank God for those people, they probably saved my life and if I didn't thank them then, I want to now. They must have thought I was crazy.

We arrived at Mercy Hospital and once again the angels sent me another Peter. He was the Emergency Room physician and was very kind, trying to calm me down and trying to explain everything as he examined me. Ellen was there holding my hand and giving me reassurances. The monitors that I was hooked up to were behind me and I couldn't see the numbers but she could. The doctor looked at my feet and saw that they were all puffed up and swollen and it was then, the first time I heard the word 'heart' spoken. Ellen was reading the chart and told me that my problem was not asthma but congestive heart failure. "What in the hell is that" I asked? Dr. Peter explained to me why I was having so much trouble breathing; that it was a serious condition and that he was going to admit me to the hospital. Then, as if a veil was lifted, I could draw a deep breath. I don't know if it was a medication they had given me or if I had just calmed down and stopped fighting and started accepting, but I could breath.

"You are really sick, Jacqui," Ellen said and I told her I didn't care how sick I was, I could breathe. After weeks of fighting for breath, this was the first relief I had had. It was a release from bondage and fear.

The next thing I knew I was in a room and wearing one of those flattering jonnies. They brought in this gigantic bag and catheterized me and I proceeded to fill that bag within hours. I never thought a body could hold so much fluid but that is what happens when you have congestive heart failure. Then, here come the needles. I had needle tracks in my arms and hands; all over my body eventually. Now, here comes the parade of doctors and every conceivable test that was ever devised. They were all cardiologists and the one that was assigned to me was Dr. Lisa Thomas. Dr. Thomas explained that my heart had gone through tremendous struggles to get the blood back to the heart but the congestion was preventing it from happening. She said that they were going to have to take a look at what was going on.

The next morning I was taken to an examining room with all kinds of curious equipment. Dr. Thomas explained that they were going to go into the large artery of my groin and send a catheter that would travel through my body to my heart and would show the problem areas. The procedure started and as far as I know I had no pain. We all watched the procedure on a television-like screen and it was fascinating to watch.

They were a team of real professionals who talked to me and to each other as they proceeded. They showed me the places where cholesterol had built up in my arteries. Those places showed up as definite congested areas of the blood vessel and they explained that it was these areas that were causing all my problems. It was an enthralling afternoon until they told me that I was to have quadruple by-pass surgery.

Ellen had contacted Velicia to fill her in on what was happening and she made immediate plane reservations to come be with me. She walked through the door of my room and came to me with a big hug. She was so good to me. She stayed at my house and visited daily as we walked through the valley of heart surgery.

One day 'God' walked into my room. He was this tall, handsome man with the brightest smile you ever saw; the whitest teeth and the blackest skin in the world. I looked at him again and almost fainted. He had been a student of mine at the Portland Conservatory. I knew he was a doctor but I had no idea he was a cardiac surgeon. "What are you doing here Dr. Braxton?" I asked in utter amazement.

"No, no" he responded, "What are you doing here?" He took my hand in his and pulled up a chair to my bed and looked me right in the eyes and said, "We are going to fix this." He explained that I would be moved from Mercy Hospital to Maine Medical Center because that is where the necessary equipment was and also that was where his office was. He didn't to go into the details of a quadruple bypass but said that he was going to do the work and he had done many of them and very successfully. I was not to worry.

Ellen and Velicia were notifying everyone that the open-heart surgery was to be that Tuesday and that I was being transferred to Maine Medical Center. The trip to Maine Med was a trip to remember. There were a bunch of EMTs in the ambulance and I told them the story about the lady who physically fought the oxygen because she couldn't breathe. They all laughed and said that they had some stories of their own. I asked them to thank those who had helped me and they said they would if they could but it was all part of the job.

Maine Medical Center is a very professional place and the people on staff were very kind and attentive. All the tests were performed with little fanfare and Tuesday was approaching rapidly. Tuesday arrived and the sequence of events started early in the morning to prepare me for one of the major happenings of my life. My only discomforts were the needles in my hands where the drips were dripping. I remember talking with the fellow who was taking me to the operating room and feeling quite drowsy and calm. I don't know but I think there was something in that drip they didn't tell me about. I had a brief glimpse of the operating room and that was all I remember.

Ellen and Velicia were waiting for me as I returned to my room from the recovery room. All had gone well and Dr. Braxton was happy that the whole procedure had gone as planned without any complications. He was urging me to go to a rehab clinic but I was very reluctant. I wanted to go home where everything was mine and I had Baby with me. I didn't want to go to some strange place where sick little ladies were walking the hallways pushing their intravenous bottles. That would only make me sicker. The nurses had me up immediately walking my own hallway and after three days I convinced them that I would be better off at home. Convincing Ellen and Velicia was another matter but in the end I won out...... and I'm still here.

I took my long list of do's and don'ts and Ellen carried the floral shop load of flowers and we went home. Velicia had gone home the day before as she had to be at work so it was just Ellen and me. I was oh so tired and the tearful trip up the back stairs was a slow and arduous task. But, dear God was it wonderful to see my house again. I went immediately to my bedroom without even looking at Baby. For some reason I couldn't face her. I guess I had to wait until we were all alone. Ellen left to check in at home and I slept a very deep sleep. When I awoke, I went into the living room and looked at Baby. She looked so good and my tears flowed so hard I was afraid I was going to stain her ebony skin. I rubbed my hands all over her and spoke soft words to her and in the depths of my imagination I felt she was as happy as I.

With a great deal of thanks to the visiting nurses and my good attitude, my recovery was rapid and complete in a matter of weeks. My strength was returning and as soon as I could sit upright at my piano, I set some timetables for returning to work. The realization of overcoming such a horrendous setback caused me to reflect upon my life as a whole and I soon discovered that I had changed. I had turned seventy years old and for the first time in my life I became aware of age. Before, age meant nothing to me because I could do all the things I ever wanted to do, but now, after this heart surgery, I am even more dedicated to continue playing my piano as long as these hands, these eyes and this heart can continue.

Throughout my life I made some very bad people mistakes and they all came back to haunt and hurt me. But now all those negative people in my life, those I had to run from, meant nothing any more; I make much better decisions than ever before. I now treasure and nurture each day as it comes; there is no bad weather; there is no gloom.

Epilogue

The day was sultry but beautiful which was typical of Maine in August. The concert was to be held that evening at the South Portland Concert Hall. I was ready and so was Jeffrey Ertmann, my glorious concert trombonist whom I would be accompanying. You see, I know that Jeffrey was sent to me; he was sent by my long lost Peter Lancto. They are so much alike that even Jeffrey's trombone has a similar sound as Peter's tuba. I know it is probably just my imagination but I swear their voices are even the same. We play as if we were one and every time we play together, I realize partially why I am here. Tonight would be no exception.

I have students today and little Dana is sitting at the piano and her grey-blue eyes penetrate mine as I outline what she should be doing. Dana accepts instruction so well that very little has to be repeated. She starts to play and my hand instinctively reaches to her shoulder. That is how I teach emotionally. If she seems too fast or slow, I can change the tempo with a tap of my finger or I can sing the music along with her play. In every case I try to paint music pictures to bring out that inner person who I know is in there. It is magic to see talent like hers and my soul gets stirred when I recognize it. The beauty of it all is when students like this realize that I see the potential. It is then that they want what I want for them. My students are not all like little Dana but they all get the same Jacqueline Gourdin.

This evening the hall is nicely crowded and I swear that everyone I love is there. Someone is setting up for recording the performance and the programs are waving to cool summer faces. My Jeffrey is this big, tall young man who is as big a soul as he is a presence. When you play with your soul-mate, you truly become one; musically and spiritually. The minute his lips touch the mouthpiece and my fingers touch the keys, we don't have to worry about each other; it just happens and the music flows from our depths. It is the pleasure of this that has consumed my life. It is the raison d'etre that has allowed me to overcome all the negatives of existence. My piano speaks to me of other times; other days in a way that erases all hurt and fear. My piano is me.

The concert is over and the people stand to tell us how much they appreciate what we have done. Ellen stands with Brenda and Bob and the smiles on their faces show me the love they have for me. I am ecstatic with joy and as everyone sits for our encore, I move to the microphone and there is a deafening silence because this is something that doesn't normally happen. "Thank you ladies and gentlemen," I begin. "There is a man here tonight who I want you all to know and to whom this concert is dedicated. He is a man who has renewed my life; a man of such towering strength and tenderness whom I will never be able to thank enough and whom I will never forget. This man is Dr. John Braxton, my cardiac surgeon who has literally held my heart in his hands. Please stand Doctor and I want everyone here to know how much I love you."

Embarrassed but smiling, he stands and the audience applauds with thunder. When calm was restored I go on to say, "You should also know that Dr. Braxton is once again one of my students and is doing the five finger exercises with the rest of them." The laughter was light and cathartic and then I announced the final number of the evening, George Gershwin's, "Someone To Watch Over Me. "

The reception was over and I sat alone at the piano bench reflecting on the day. Jeff had gone and Dr. Braxton had gone and I was overcome with the feeling that truly someone was watching over me; now and had throughout all the years. How had people like these come into my life? The only thing that had been a constant was my piano. Everything had come to me through my piano since I was that little girl in the pinafore. I was dedicated to finding my father but somehow I never discovered him in a physical manner and yet through all my trials and difficulties; and during the good times too, I felt his presence. It was then I realized that he showed himself through my piano. It was his way of materializing his love and guidance for me. I am so different from anyone else in my family, I must be like him. I left the empty hall with a new sense of discovery. I knew that he had been revealing himself to me through Baby; through my piano. Thank you Daddy. I laughed a little laugh, picked up my music and went home…to play.